the

MOMINATRIX'S
GUIDE TO SEX

A NO-SURRENDER ADVICE BOOK

for

NAUGHTY MOMS

KRISTEN CHASE

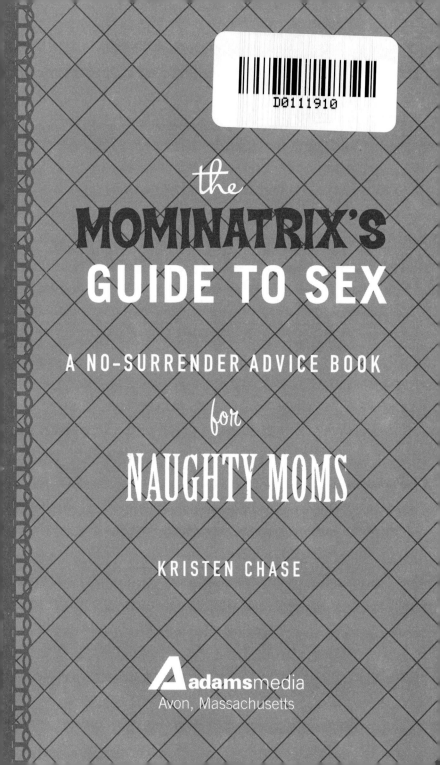

Adamsmedia
Avon, Massachusetts

For Quinlan, Drew, and Margot,
the best three things I ever got out of sex.

And for my husband, with whom sex made
me a mom in the first place.

Published by
Adams Media, a division of F+W Media, Inc.
57 Littlefield Street, Avon, MA 02322. U.S.A.
www.adamsmedia.com

ISBN 10: 1-60550-361-4
ISBN 13: 978-1-60550-361-5

Printed in the United States of America.

10 9 8 7 6 5 4 3 2 1

Library of Congress Cataloging-in-Publication Data
is available from the publisher.

This publication is designed to provide accurate and authoritative information
with regard to the subject matter covered. It is sold with the understanding that
the publisher is not engaged in rendering legal, accounting, or other professional
advice. If legal advice or other expert assistance is required, the services of a
competent professional person should be sought.
—From a *Declaration of Principles* jointly adopted by a Committee of the
American Bar Association and a Committee of Publishers and Associations

Many of the designations used by manufacturers and sellers to distinguish their
product are claimed as trademarks. Where those designations appear in this
book and Adams Media was aware of a trademark claim, the designations have
been printed with initial capital letters.

This book is available at quantity discounts for bulk purchases.
For information, please call 1-800-289-0963.

"For naughty moms indeed! Even though my twins were born almost two years ago, my sex life has not been what it used to be. This fun, frank, and raunchy book was just the kick in the pants I needed—encouraging me to spice things up. *The Mominatrix's Guide to Sex* is my new dirty little secret!"

—Stefanie Wilder-Taylor, author of *Sippy Cups Are Not for Chardonnay: And Other Things I Had to Learn as a New Mom*

"Chase has penned a thoroughly honest, hilarious, and insightful 'I've-been-there-too' book for partners who become parents and want to do whatever is needed to keep their adult relationship, aka sex lives, intact. If you like sex, this is an in-the-trenches report that will validate your experiences, make you laugh, and guide you through the tumult of attaining your own personally declared Mominatrix status."

—Lou Paget, sexpert and bestselling author of *How to Be a Great Lover*

"Kristen Chase is right: It's not a good idea to Google 'moms with questions about sex.' And thanks to her book, you don't have to. *The Mominatrix's Guide to Sex* has all the answers, whether you've just found out you're pregnant or you're locking the kiddies out of your bedroom. Of course, you'll want to hide her guide for 'naughty moms' once the kids learn to read. . . ."

—Jen Singer, creator of MommaSaid.net and author of the *Stop Second-Guessing Yourself* guides to parenting

"A must-read for every tired new mom who fears her sex life will remain a distant memory."

—Amy Keroes, CEO, *www.mommytracked.com*

"The grind of daily life may have drained the "sexy mama" right out of you, but Kristen Chase is there to tell you how to find it, reclaim it, and thoroughly enjoy it."

— Adrienne Hedger, author and illustrator of *If These Boobs Could Talk* and *Momnesia*

"A sensitive, frank, and funny-as-hell guide for new parents. *The Mominatrix's Guide to Sex* offers tons of practical, parent-friendly tips to kick-start your libido after having a baby."

— Heather Gibbs Flett, coauthor of *The Rookie Mom's Handbook* and cofounder of RookieMoms.com

"Attention mothers of planet earth: Even if you already know your way around a string of anal beads (and God bless you if you do), you need to read this book. Kristen Chase is savvy, funny, and brutally honest—a refreshing new voice that bends over the often-prudish notion of parental sex and smacks it on the ass."

— Danny Evans, author of *Rage Against the Meshugenah: Why It Takes Balls to Go Nuts*

"Whether you're in the market to expand your sexual horizons or recharge your bedroom batteries, Kristen Chase's *The Mominatrix's Guide to Sex* is sure to entice and motivate all Mominatrix(es)-in-training. An uncensored, no-holds-barred, in-your-face, ass-slapping romp. Oh, baby."

— Rebecca Woolf, author of *Rockabye: From Wild to Child*

CONTENTS

ACKNOWLEDGMENTS

Special thanks to Prescott and Jessica Carlson from ImperfectParent.com, for picking me to write the *Mominatrix* column and ignoring my lame titles; to Holly Schmidt, for thinking the column had the potential to become a book; to Jennster and Kristin Darzugas, for sharing their experiences as single moms; to Asha Dornfest, Rita Arens, Rebecca Woolf, Julie Marsh, and Liz Gumbinner, for their guidance, friendship, and answers to my frantic e-mails throughout this process; to my dear friend Tina, for making my funny even funnier; and to my fellow blogging moms and readers, for listening to my rants, getting my jokes, and giving me your virtual shoulders (and favorite movie sex scenes) when I needed them most. Here's to never leaving our libidos at the hospital or tossing them out with the dirty diapers.

INTRODUCTION

When you are expecting, that pregnant belly you're boasting is probably the most obvious physical evidence that you've been having sex. Nothing says "I'm doing it" like a knocked-up mommy.

So then why do pregnant moms become painted as desexualized robots concerned only with baby names and nursery bedding? And why does this stigma continue after the baby is born? Suddenly, you're supposed to be satisfied by wiping your baby's butt and changing spit-soaked bibs all day long. You've left your libido at the hospital and your days as a sex goddess are supposed to be history. At least, that's what all the experts would have you think.

Unless you're a silicone-pumped MILF or a young, careless celebrity mommy, no one does a double take at the postpartum mom in yoga pants wiping spit-up and drool off a shirt she's worn for the last two days. Go figure.

And so the act that got many of you into parenthood in the first place is put on auto-drive. Load, spin, and repeat—if you're lucky. Laundry sex. It's all the rage.

When you bring home a baby, your sexuality doesn't just magically disappear to make room for the extra hormones and breastmilk. It just shifts to the back burner—you know, after the kids are asleep, the dishes are done, and you've lost the extra cellulite off the back of your thighs. Or at least until you've figured out a way to strategically cover it up.

The desire and the hunger are generally salvageable, except now they require a little more than the simple "meal" that used to satisfy them, and a little more prep time than a TV dinner. Clearly, the passing smooch and the half-assed hand job just don't cut it anymore.

So where do you go when you're ready to amp things up? Go ahead and Google "mom with questions about sex." The five hundred pay-to-play porn sites just don't seem like the best solution.

And really, the last thing you probably want to do with your free 4.5 minutes between feedings and laundry loads is to surf questionable Internet sites for new and exciting positions and techniques. No mom, new or not, needs to see some scantily clad skinny girl who hasn't had anyone younger than 22 suck on her boobs getting banged with her legs wrapped behind her head. That stuff might have done the trick a few years ago, but no perky-breasted twenty-something can help you deal with what motherhood has done to your sex life.

You're busy, you're tired, and you're dealing with one of those teeny tiny humans who have the insane ability to suck, chew, and spit out every last bit of your soul in a way that just makes you love them more. And while you'd love to spend a long evening of romance being wooed by your husband, you can barely get a few minutes to yourself, let alone an hour. Plus, he hasn't changed a diaper in a week, he just got back from a business trip where he ate every meal peacefully alone, and he had the audacity to complain about being tired. So even if you did have the energy and motivation to hop in the sack, you'd probably prefer it to be with Brad Pitt and not your well-fed, well-rested husband who almost forgot what a diaper was.

Motherhood undoubtedly affects your sex life, but with little impetus to explore the new changes in your body and sexual being, you focus your attention on those who need it most—your kids. You feed them mashed organic bananas and dress them in über boutique couture. Meanwhile, you're eating perpetual leftovers and walking around like a zombie in a baseball cap.

Still, while their tummies are pesticide-free and their butts are covered in designer duds, it might be nice if someone cared about your stomach and ass just as much. But if the only vibe you're sending out is "I haven't showered since last Tuesday," you can't expect your partner to jump you on the couch.

That doesn't mean you should beat yourself up over your greasy head and hairy pits. Even the best of mothers have forgone simple pleasures like washing their hair and shaving their underarms as they adapt to the complicated schedule of life with kids. But they are babies after all—the wet diaper can wait a few minutes so you can put on some makeup and an outfit actually made to be worn outside and not to bed.

For a mother regaining her sexual self, it's way less about learning the latest and greatest blowjob technique and more about figuring out how to make a sexual relationship work when the batteries from your vibrator are now powering your baby monitor and the last orgasm you had was when your baby slept four hours in a row.

Maybe the only adjustment you'll have to make to your sex life is remembering to lock your door. But some of you might have to relearn *everything* you once knew. Having babies really does change everything, and as frustrating as it might be to have to figure yet another thing out, it shouldn't really be that big of a surprise. You already expanded and retracted your waistline and turned your house upside down. Maybe you even bought a new car. What's a few changes in the bedroom department?

When it comes to reorienting and rejuvenating your libido, you probably don't want any more dry technical advice or helpful hints from experts who just want to send you on date nights or make you fill out a foreplay map. Sure, it's not a bad idea to get out of the house without the kids on a regular basis and to reassess your bedroom antics, but you probably don't need some random doctor to tell you that.

Motherhood is hard enough—with strangers judging your every move and everyone telling you what you should be doing better—so there's no reason to subject yourself to any more torture than you already endure on a daily basis. Your kids may have taken over most of your life, but you're still the mistress of your own domain. The Mominatrix is here to help you get back what's rightfully yours. So get ready to toss out that ratty bra and retire those mommy jeans. Just be careful with that whip.

1

SEX AND THE PREGNANT WOMAN

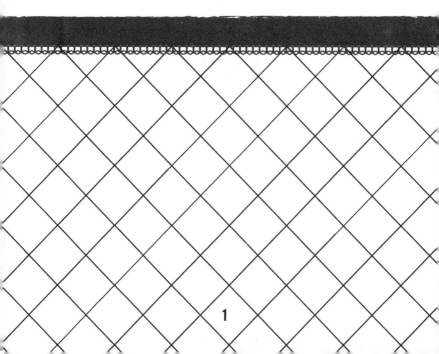

Whether it took months of carefully planned baby-making sessions or one drunken, spontaneous, condom-breaking sexcapade, you're approximately ten months away (yes, ten) from becoming a mom.

Cue angels singing.

Or wait, is that you screeching?

These next forty-plus weeks will not only wreak varying levels of havoc on your poor unsuspecting body, but on your sex life as well. That's not to say you won't be one of that rare strain of preggos who have a total life-changing sexual awakening in their whale-like state. Maybe you have been chosen by the great pregnancy gods to bust that urban myth.

For most pregnant women, however, sex during pregnancy can be a tricky beast. By the time you're feeling rested enough to actually try, you're too big and uncomfortable to actually enjoy it. But feeling great about your changing body will help make pregnancy sex as hot as it can possibly be. And loving every inch of you—regardless of how many zits, stretch marks, and varicose veins you end up with—will help take your mind off all the crazy stuff that comes with being a breeder.

And it certainly can't hurt whatever sex you might already be having.

But basking in your new pregnancy body is a little easier said than done. For the first few months, you're bloated, tired, and spending way too much time in the bathroom, which doesn't translate to "sexy" in any language. And once you're visibly pregnant, well, you're visibly pregnant. Whether you've just gained enough weight to look like you've got a basketball under your shirt, or you look like you're carrying twins, it's a difficult adjustment for any woman.

DOING A PREGNANT BODY GOOD

These days, you are by no means the only visible woman in the world reproducing. Thanks to a slew of breeding celebrities, having a baby has now become the next "it" thing. And while baby making is by no means a trend, you'll find a ridiculous number of websites, magazines, and even movies that suggest otherwise.

In other words, thanks to the popularity of pregnancy, you'll find no shortage of various products that will promise to do almost anything to help you adjust to your new pregnant self. The manufacturers know that you're tired, impulsive, and desperate for anything that promises to make you feel both human and mom-like. Apparently, they hope that little fetus growing inside you makes you a big sucker.

But as with anything else, when a trend is identified, people are quick to make "must-have" products to hawk to that specific group. And no surprise, many of these products are a total scam, completely frivolous, or definitely not a "must-have."

Now early on, most preggos are looking for anything other than the inside of the toilet bowl to make them feel like they are pregnant. As a result, you'll be bombarded with the words *stretch marks* even before you've gained a pound, and you'll find yourself shopping for maternity shirts even though your baby is the size of a peanut.

Later, when you reach the stage when you might actually have a need for belly lotions and walrus-sized maternity shirts, you'll be tempted with products to make you feel less pregnant and more human—like skin-tightening natural lotions and sexy dresses that you can wear after the baby comes. Because that's exactly what you'll feel like wearing with your maxi pads and nursing bra, right? A sexy dress. How thoughtful of them to make something so useful.

And if that's not confusing enough, throughout your pregnancy everyone will offer their opinion about how much you should be eating, how much weight you shouldn't be gaining, and everything in between. People you don't even know will stop you on the street to discuss your pregnancy diet like they're your personal physician.

"You're not really eating for two," the strangers at the next booth will tell you as they shove gigantic bowls of pasta down their own gullets. "That's just a myth; you don't really need any extra calories." *Um, thanks. Now pass the doughnuts.*

MOMINATRIX SAYS

Yes, it's true. Stretch marks are completely genetic. That doesn't mean there's no hope for you. Drink lots of water, keep your belly moisturized, and cross your fingers. If that's not enough, snag a few products from Mama Mio *www.mamamio.com*. They're good enough for J.Lo, so who knows, right?

But when it comes down to it, you'll need to use your own judgment. Make sure you don't buy a pregnancy remedy or follow someone else's advice simply because you're afraid you'll end up with a stomach covered in stretch marks. Instead, do it only if it really does make you feel better. If your ass truly looks smaller thanks to that special expensive lotion, then buy it. Follow your own instinct and you'll be fine.

For all women, pregnant or not, feeling sexy is about being comfortable in our own skin. And although your skin happens to be growing and stretching to almost incomprehensible sizes, there are plenty of ways for you to still feel great about your new body and changing self.

Sure, beauty comes from within. But if you can't get past the new body, you'll never be able to actually work on the inside. So regardless of what you purchase or whom you listen to, here are a few things to consider when you're trying to feel sexy as a newly pregnant person.

Lotions and Potions

There's no shortage of various creams and other skincare products that claim to help reduce or even eliminate stretch marks. Of course, the catch is that if you use them and you don't get stretch marks, you'll never know if the cream stopped them or if you just have some damn good genes.

Throughout your pregnancy, you'll be inundated with miracle foot soaks, belly balms, and every single imaginable product in between, with claims to shrink your feet and keep your ass from widening. As tempting as it might seem, particularly if you're already distraught over your body's changes, don't buy into the hype. In most cases, your body's reaction to or acceptance of pregnancy is completely genetic and won't be affected by a lotion.

That doesn't mean you don't deserve some pampering. In fact, you might just find that taking the time to enjoy whatever products you purchase gives you an excuse to focus on yourself for even a few minutes out of your very busy day. And if you feel better rubbing a magic pregnancy potion on your belly three times a day, then there's probably no harm in trying a few out.

But until they invent a cream that keeps people from touching your belly or gets you into your pre-pregnancy jeans before you leave the hospital, then you might want to save your cash for more useful items, like an epidural.

Diet and Exercise

In most cases, it's perfectly safe to exercise and eat well during your pregnancy. In fact, regular physical activity often helps make your pregnancy easier and your labor and delivery faster. Aside from keeping away from the typical no-noes that your doctor or midwife will surely scare you about, maintaining some type of physical activity and a healthy diet can help your self-esteem and sex life. Just make sure to get your exercise plan approved by a health professional, particularly if you're at high risk or you haven't exercised in a while. Clearly now is not the time to train for a marathon or, in some cases, even a 5K run, but a daily walk or trot on the treadmill can promote a speedy postpartum recovery. And it can help work off the box of Ho-Hos you ate for breakfast the other day.

MOMINATRIX **SAYS**

Not only is sex way more interesting than walking on the treadmill, but it burns about 65 calories per half hour. Don't gawk—it'll take you that long to change positions, so you could be looking at a good hour of exercise per sex session.

When it comes to food, don't guilt yourself into oblivion if you develop some ridiculous Taco Bell addiction. Babies can survive in utero on French fries and burritos alone. Plus, you'll have enough to feel bad about after the baby arrives. However, most pregnancy nutrition programs encourage moms to eat lots of protein and folic acid, along with fresh veggies and whole grains. Stick to the four major food groups as best you can, but don't feel bad about indulging yourself when you feel the urge—even if that urge will only be satisfied by an Oreo Blizzard. And make sure to pop those prenatal vitamins.

MOMINATRIX SAYS

There are specific foods that pregnant women should avoid, including tuna, soft unpasteurized cheeses, raw fish and eggs. You'll also want to be sure to microwave or heat lunch meats. For a complete list, talk to your doctor or midwife.

Unders and Outers

Even with a rapidly growing belly, there's really no reason to purchase special maternity bras and panties. If you find that your regular-sized undergarments get a bit tight at some point—whether it's during the first or last few weeks of your pregnancy—don't feel as though you need to be relegated to gigantic windsock underpants from your local maternity shop. Instead, grab your favorite underwear in a size (or two) up, or explore some different styles that might not irritate your belly or get stuck in your new sizable ass.

Thanks to the popularity of low riders, you'll be able to find plenty of under-the-belly options right at your favorite lingerie shops. And if those don't work, there's nothing sexier than going commando or—for pregnant women—"ready for labor."

When it comes to clothing, you'll be pleased to find that maternity wear has gotten increasingly stylish over the years. So even if you don't feel sexy in your own skin at the moment, you can find clothes to help ease the transition.

If you're not sporting a belly just yet, you can certainly find great size-up regular clothes that will fit you. Unless you're trying to hide the fact that you're pregnant, there's no excuse for walking around in a tent. Besides, wearing a tent generally screams "pregnant" even without the belly. That being said, don't stuff yourself into clothes that just don't fit you anymore. Also remember that it's hard to predict what size you'll need a few months down the road, so shop often and buy only what works on your current body.

Fit is important, especially when it comes to maternity clothes. The last thing you need is to be constantly hiking up your pants or pulling down your shirt. It's hard to predict what size you'll need a few months down the road, even with that fake belly strapped around your waist.

MOMINATRIX SAYS

The whole "buy your pre-pregnancy size" is a bunch of bullshit, mostly because it does not account for any extra weight you might now be carrying. (Hello thighs and butt!) So try things on, and don't freak yourself out if you're a size or two up from your normal size.

And since you definitely get what you pay for in terms of quality, consider shelling out a few extra bucks for more expensive, well-made staple pieces that will last you through your entire pregnancy. Toward the end, you may even fit into only one or two items that you'll wash and wear every day until that baby finally makes an entrance. Save the cheap T-shirts and tent-like skirts for the last month or so of your pregnancy. You'll probably never wear them again anyway. And thank goodness for that.

You certainly don't need some slinky maternity dress to feel sexy. On the contrary, a hot pair of jeans and a slim-fitting T-shirt can have the same effect. And if you shop well, particularly when it comes to second-trimester clothing, you'll have a bunch of great pieces that you can wear during those first few postpartum months.

THE MOMINATRIX'S TOP THREE PICKS FOR SEXY MATERNITY WEAR		
Rosie Pope	*www.rosiepope.com*	Anyone who has the balls to make a backless maternity dress should be number one on your list.
Isabella Oliver	*www.isabellaoliver.com*	You'll be instantly smitten with their offering of stylish maternity clothes for day, night, and everything in between.
Chiara Kruza	*www.chiarakruza.com*	This mom and designer combines flirty and functional in clothes you'll still be able to wear into your fourth and fifth trimester.

The Nethers

Caring for your pubic hair won't be an issue until you can't see past your belly. After that, you'll want to use great caution, unless you're skilled at caring for your pubes without actually being able to see them.

While you should be able to continue your grooming routine through the first few months, when you're unable to actually see your nether regions, you should pass the duty on to someone else—either a paid professional or a skilled partner.

MOMINATRIX SAYS

Contrary to old medical practices, a trim or shaved crotch doesn't necessarily make it easier for your doctor or midwife to see what's going on down there during labor. But it might make you feel better, and these days, that's a perfectly good reason to keep things maintained down below.

Keep in mind that you're going to be more sensitive down there, so make sure to practice your deep yoga breaths during your next wax appointment, or just ask your esthetician to tame your crotch without sending you into premature labor.

If your partner is nimble with a pair of scissors and a razor, then it's a perfect opportunity to enlist his assistance in the upkeep. And when done well, beaver trimming can always be a nice prelude to sex.

WHAT TO EXPECT IN THE BEDROOM WHEN YOU'RE EXPECTING

Now that you've spiffed yourself up, you might want to get the full skinny on how sex plays out during pregnancy. Granted you've probably got baby names and bathtubs on your brain, but after you've figured out a moniker and what ridiculously overpriced plastic container you'll bathe Junior in, you're still a woman with needs.

You'll get more than enough of the weekly play-by-play when it comes to your fetus and your own body in the plethora of pregnancy books you've got stacked on your nightstand or piled high on the bathroom floor, so here's an idea of what things will look like in the sex department based on the pregnancy trimesters.

The First Twelve Weeks: Welcome to the Jungle

During the first trimester, the amount of sex you have (or better, the number of times the idea of sex actually enters your head), greatly depends on how much of your breakfast—or if you're really bad off, lunch and dinner—you're able to hold down. Add in migraines, exhaustion, and a plethora of symptoms that don't tend to scream "come hither" and you've probably got anything but sex on your mind.

MOMINATRIX SAYS

If you have a history of miscarriage or any type of early pregnancy condition, make sure to check with your doctor or midwife before going at it.

For the most part, the first trimester will slow you down (some of you more than others), so be prepared for your sex life to pop into a lower gear. It's pretty challenging to get it on when you're passed out on the couch or munching on saltines chased with ginger ale. Also, if you tried really hard to conceive, to the point where sex became more of a chore and duty than a spontaneous pleasurable experience, then you and your partner are probably enjoying the little break from your Boot Camp of Sex regimen.

If you do happen to feel hungry for sex, then you should know it's perfectly safe during the first trimester. Contrary to your partner's concern about his gigantic hose of a penis, he will not be able to knock the baby loose. And while you might roll your eyes at the idea of some idiot actually thinking that, you'd be surprised to know how many guys believe that it's possible. Aside from not understanding that most pregnant women's cervixes are closed tighter than Fort Knox, they're probably a bit misinformed about their penis size. Don't burst their bubble. Just tell your partner that your cervix is there for a reason and feel free to bang away.

Whether it took you daily sex for more than a year to get pregnant or just one random try, don't feel bad if you'd prefer to let the memory of that sex get you through the next twelve weeks. Grab a copy of *Playboy* for your hubby and some Vaseline, paste your picture over all the faces, and go to sleep.

Preferred Sexual Positions: Anything that allows you to get long hours of uninterrupted sleep should be in the stars of your first-trimester repertoire. Get some rest and save your energy for the second trimester.

Partner Reaction: Your partner will probably be excited, overwhelmed, and maybe even a bit sympathy-sick. It might be difficult for him to fathom the changes your body is going through, particularly since there really isn't anything visibly different about you—except for all the time you're spending in bed or hovering over the pregnancy books. Just keep him as involved and informed as you can, even if that means asking him to eat his meals in another room. And reassure him that if you actually do feel like having sex, you'll be sure to let him know.

The Second-Trimester Epiphany

The majority of pregnant women see a definite shift from bloated vomitous alien takeover to fully fledged glowing pregnant mother-to-be when they hit sixteen weeks. Or eighteen weeks. Or sometime before the baby comes.

Okay, really, it's true. You're supposed to be less tired once you hit the second trimester, and many women do report an amazing shift in their overall demeanor.

You might actually have a bit of a baby belly showing, which makes life a little easier when it comes to dealing with your new expanding waist (and ass, depending on your luck of the draw). Dealing with the first-trimester bloat can be pretty annoying, but the cute baby bump makes the unbuttoned pants bearable during the second stage.

MOMINATRIX SAYS

If your partner gets weirded out when he feels the baby move during sex, consider positions where he can't get kicked by the baby. Reverse cowboy or side by side are two good options.

And the best part is that you might even feel like having sex. In fact, you might even feel like having sex a lot.

All those hormones coursing through your veins start to make your special parts become extra sensitive. Many women report that their sexual experience is magnified thanks to extra blood to the vaginal area. And since you're only the size of a studio apartment and not a gigantic four-bedroom just yet, you can still move around pretty freely and enjoy yourself without having to drag around all the extra baggage.

So definitely consider translating those crazy-hot pregnancy dreams into reality and take advantage of the second-trimester window of opportunity. Think of it as having a vibrator permanently attached to your clitoris.

Since the last trimester tends to slow down moms-to-be in more ways than one, enjoy it while you can. Plus it'll take your mind off the fact that in a few short months, you'll have to get that baby out of your vagina.

Preferred Sexual Positions: Since you're already pregnant, have some crazy monkey sex in whatever position you like before you hit the beached-whale trimester. Get it while you can and while you still actually want and like it.

Partner Reaction: Your partner is bound to feel better right along with you. And your surge of energy might generate a revitalized sex life. Your growing baby and cute belly can make things a bit more exciting, mainly because your partner can be more actively involved in the pregnancy now that he can actually "see" the baby. Even though your belly isn't big enough to interfere with certain positions, partners can get a little freaked out when they feel the baby move during sex. Use your best distraction techniques and refocus him on the prize before it's too late.

The Third Trimester: The Final Countdown

Don't get too used to the glorious glow because the third trimester will wipe it right off your big swollen face.

And the excitement that comes with being near the end is dashed not only by your growing discomfort, but also by that looming thing called *labor.*

Clearly, sex would be a fantastic distraction if it was actually comfortable, but most moms will attest to the fact that at some point during the third trimester you'll end up requiring large machinery to get you from the bed to the bathroom every two hours. A fun lighthearted romp in the sack is probably not in the cards.

There are some women who do report that the second-trimester sexual high continues right through until the birth of their baby. Keeping fit as well as maintaining a healthy weight can certainly help make the sex just as hot.

Unfortunately, no amount of working out will change the fact that you've got a baby pressing squarely on your cervix. As you might guess, having a baby basically hanging down between your legs can make sex pretty uncomfortable. This can be a bit frustrating for you and your partner, particularly if you were having crazy second-trimester sex and now you can't even tie your own shoes let alone climb on top of your partner for a wild ride.

You should not, however, be discouraged by your loss of agility and overall comfort in the bedroom. And don't feel relegated to giving your husband obligatory oral sex. The late-pregnancy-induced sinus issues will make that quite a challenge. However, with a couple of clever apparatus and a little creativity, you can indulge in a bit of sexual horsing around without feeling like an actual horse.

If you don't own a sex wedge, then you've now got the perfect excuse to purchase one without feeling like a sexual deviant. It'll help make certain positions more comfortable, and even make ones you thought completely off limits due to your lack of gymnastic abilities actually doable. Don't be turned off by the name; a sleep wedge will do the same exact thing, and when you're not using it for sex, you can use it as a sleeping aid (or, more likely, as a constant visual reminder of all the sleep you wish you were getting). But seriously, you'll be amazed at what a little bit of propping up and repositioning can do for your experience.

If you don't want to drop the cash on the wedge, you can actually use that nursing pillow you added to your registry. Just make sure you buy an extra cover.

THE MOMINATRIX'S TOP THREE "SEX WEDGES" (AKA NURSING PILLOWS)		
The Baby Buddy	*www.thebabybuddy.ca*	Still shaped to fit comfortably around your waist, The Baby Buddy is a bit more plush and pillow-like, making it easier to manipulate into various nursing and sexual positions.
Blessed Nest Organic Nesting Pillow	*www.blessednestperch .com*	Made from organic cotton, this pillow is filled with beans, allowing it to mold to your and your baby's body. Or your partner's, depending on how you're using it.
My Breast Friend	*www.mybrestfriend.com*	Aside from the fantastic name, this firm flat pillow provides solid support—of your baby, or your bum.

Once you're propped up and repositioned, you may find that you need a little battery-operated assistance.

Due to the baby's positioning, your experience of penetration can feel more like when your doctor inserts a speculum, so partial entry might be the way to go. Of course, trying to convince your partner to just put half his penis inside you might be a pretty daunting task. And you might find that a half dick does nothing but frustrate you and lead to a fairly uninspired experience. So consider adding a sex toy into the mix—something your partner wears or something you've already got in your nightstand drawer—to offer you some clitoral stimulation. There's a good chance that's the only way you're going to come close to orgasm.

MOMINATRIX SAYS

If you can convince your partner to wear it, a vibrating cock ring will provide you with clitoral stimulation during penetration—a bonus for both parties involved.

And never count out a regular masturbation session, either with the help of your eager partner or just on your own. Just because you don't physically enjoy intercourse doesn't mean you can't take advantage of those ridiculously raging hormones. In a matter of months you'll be losing any semblance of autonomy that you ever had, so you might as well spend as much time alone with yourself as possible. Plus it's a great way to pass the sleepless nights that have probably already started, even without the little screaming bundle of joy.

It's clear that the reason doctors recommend sex as a possible labor inducer, aside from the hormone in sperm that can soften the uterus, is because most couples probably aren't having it near their due date, so any type of action, might just start up contractions.

But given the level of discomfort associated with late-pregnancy fornication, most pregnant women may decide to go for a stroll instead.

Preferred Sexual Positions: Anything you find remotely comfortable wins—generally positions where you have control over the penetration level are best. But don't be surprised if the only positions you find enjoyable involve getting your feet rubbed while eating tubs of ice cream.

Partner Reaction: Even if your partner is horny, he'll probably be too distracted putting swings, seats, and cribs together to bug you. Of course, your pregnant glow might be enough to suck him right back in, or depending on how you're feeling, send him packing. If he can get past the gigantic belly, he's still got to deal with trying to make you comfortable. And in that case, he might just stick to painting the baby's room with a toothbrush since that's probably easier than trying to ease your aches and pains.

SPECIAL SITUATIONS: HIGH-RISK PREGNANCIES

For some women, pregnancy sex is a bit more complicated than just finding a comfortable position. And for others, it can be a matter of whether sex is actually on the menu for the next nine months or if it's been added to the forbidden list along with artisan cheeses and sushi.

If you've been awarded bed rest or labeled as "high-risk," make sure to check with your doctor about what type of sexual activity you can engage in, if any. In most cases, it's not just the physical activity that is off limits but also the actual orgasms. Since climaxing actually contracts your uterus, which opens your cervix, even masturbation can be out of the question.

Mominatrix SAYS

Missionary position is a big no-no during the latter trimesters, so if you have to be on your back consider propping yourself up with a bunch of pillows, or playing around with some other adaptations that are comfy for you and safe for baby.

Of course, it can be better to give than to receive, at least if you believe in the mantra of men everywhere, but considering that you're already giving your body and your time as you sit in a bed catching up on gossip mags, forget that rule. The only thing you should be giving right now is orders.

Still, just because you're stuck in bed doesn't mean you've got to spend your days watching soap operas and reading baby books. Keep your sexy self alive and kicking without sending yourself into labor by strategically passing the time with movies and books that will put a goofy romantic grin on your face, which is about as hot as you can get.

INFERTILE COUPLES: GETTING BACK ON THE SEX WAGON

Since sex may have become more of a household chore and less of a spontaneous, loving act between two people, many couples who have struggled with infertility find hopping back in the sack terribly complicated. Enjoying sex as a means to express intimacy and not as a way to make a baby often becomes an extremely foreign concept, and the fun, the excitement, and the mystery can be difficult to rekindle. Partner that with an air of nervousness and anxiety when it comes to the viability and sustainability of the pregnancy, and many couples do not rapidly recover.

MOMINATRIX SAYS

If you're having trouble readjusting your sex lives, pretend that you're dating again. It'll be great for your sex life and for your relationship, both of which might take a hard hit when the baby arrives.

If you're in the high-risk pregnancy category, then continue to follow your doctor's recommendations for sex. However, if the sky's the limit, then allow yourselves time to adjust back to normalcy. This might entail spending quality time together that doesn't involve talking about the baby. Challenging as this might be, it's important that you grow your relationship back to a place where everything does not revolve around getting pregnant. Over time, the love and attention you share will heal all sexual wounds. Besides, as a parent, you'll have enough time to worry about life. So do what you can now to enjoy it as two people in love.

Regardless of whether sex is completely forbidden or open for business, it's important throughout your pregnancy to redevelop how you relate to each other sexually, even if it's just through tender kissing and simple fore-play. After all, considering what's about to happen to your lives, you will need to work as a well-oiled, lubed-up team whenever possible.

2

YOUR FIRST TIME (NO, NOT THAT ONE!)

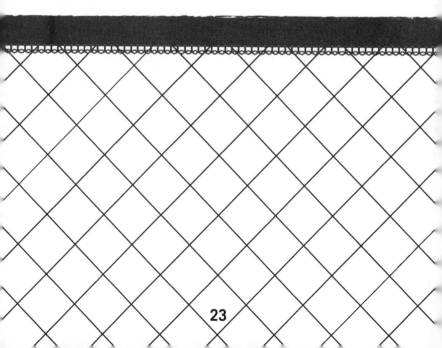

Regardless of whether you pushed that baby out of your nether regions or had Junior surgically removed from your uterus, the last thing any new mom wants to discuss is sex. In fact, most moms would probably rather be asked about how their baby is sleeping or whether they've lost all the baby weight yet than talk about having sex again.

It's not just that you're probably feeling the most unsexy that you've ever felt, courtesy of gigantic maxi pads, flaring hemorrhoids, and a belly that still looks like it has a baby in it. But thinking about sex means dealing with your poor taxed vagina. Truth is, as a new mom you already have so much to worry about—managing that little alien-like creature who does nothing but suck your energy and fluids dry, and adapting to one-minute shower and potty breaks with a screaming baby—that sex probably doesn't cross your mind on a daily basis, if ever at all.

But inevitably, a horny partner at the end of his very long rope and obviously drunk on sleep deprivation and poopy diapers will try to make a move to which you will respond, "You want to put *what* in my *what*?" Then he will quickly slink away, saving his penis from shrinking anymore than it already has, and wait.

That's not to say that some mothers aren't ready to have someone other than their babies attached to their boobs, but clearly the first postpartum romp in the sheets should be taken with extra tender-loving care and be done completely on your own terms.

THE TWO POSTPARTUM SEX CAMPS

While you might think that there's really only one answer to that dreaded postpartum sex question, you've actually got two possible responses, both of which depend on your own pregnancy, labor and delivery, and subsequent recovery. Regardless of whether you plan on keeping your legs tightly crossed for a good few months, or you're counting the days until you can jump your partner, you should know that there's no right or wrong reaction—just the one that makes sense for your particular postpartum experience thus far. And who knows, maybe you'll even surprise yourself with your reaction.

"Oh, Hell No!"

Your first reaction when your partner asks if you're interested in having sex will probably be some form of "Oh, Hell No!" And that's if you've gotten sleep. Most of you would just as soon add a few more expletives and beat your partners off with a stick at the brief mention of any type of intercourse.

Your lack of sexual desire can stem from a variety of sources, including hormones, sleep deprivation, and emotional instability. Add the fact that you just had a baby pulled from your stomach or your vagina and the poor unsuspecting fool who dared to mention the idea of anything but an ice pack, and some toilet paper going near your lower half could find himself in danger of some physical harm.

Whether you were a glowing, glamorous preggo or the one who was convinced that your body had single-handedly been taken over by a brain-sucking alien, the only "sex" you can probably think about now is the gender of your sweet infant—clearly not about the kind of sex that got you into this situation in the first place.

It's not to say the thought of sex won't ever cross your mind, but it might be something you save until your child's first birthday celebration. Or high school graduation.

"Yes, Please"

For some of you, the super *take-me-home-Jesus* sex that everyone talks about as being the one saving pregnancy grace was more like an old wives' tale or urban myth. Thanks to the large belly, ligament pains, and four thousand other pregnancy-induced ailments that couldn't be further from sexy, the act of intercourse felt more like getting a vaginal exam with a paper towel roll than anything remotely pleasurable.

So, when the baby finally made its most timely exit, sex wasn't necessarily the first thing on the top of your to-do list, but it wasn't on the bottom either. The idea of being able to roll around in the sheets without the help of a crane and enjoy the forbidden "missionary position" is titillating, even to a mom whose days and nights are running together like a bad movie marathon.

Of course, you probably didn't realize there were actually two answers to the blessed question of doom because most moms who can't wait to hop back into the sex don't generally discuss it, mostly for fear that they'll be seen as freaks. Plus, if there's anything most newly postpartum moms don't discuss, sex is probably number one on a long list of "off-limit" topics. Besides, you're too busy trying to figure out how to get your boobs to work to talk about how much you wish your partner would bend you over the kitchen counter for a quickie.

So while you might feel a bit embarrassed to be thinking about your partner's butt when apparently all you should be thinking about is your baby's, it's not that uncommon for women to be ready to shed their new role of mommy for a little fun as their former self, if only for a few minutes. And considering it might have been a while since sex actually happened, and you're probably trying to fit it in between poops and feedings, a few minutes is probably a more than realistic expectation.

TELLTALE SIGNS YOU'RE READY TO HAVE SEX AGAIN

There's not a pregnancy book out there that doesn't fail to mention and discuss, sometimes at length, the six-week postpartum recovery period. If you happened to miss that part of the book, then you'll most likely get the speech from your doctor or midwife during those long last four weeks of your pregnancy about the strongly recommended six-week sexless period after the birth of your baby.

Funny thing is that you probably don't need your doctor or midwife to tell you that childbirth is a physically traumatizing event, and your body needs time to recover. Think of boot camp without the nice accommodations and sleep, with wee little babies moonlighting as staff sergeants.

You need to give your body as much rest as possible. Granted, that might be about as easy as trying to housetrain a lion, but you're just no good to anyone, most importantly your baby, if you're walking around like a zombie.

Keep in mind that the six-week window isn't for everyone, so it should not be used as a literal timetable. In fact, most midwives will schedule your postpartum gynecological visit around three to four weeks after you deliver to check in with you to see how things are going and how your body is responding to stress and lack of sleep. So instead of counting off days like a prison inmate, listen less to the generalized recommendations and more to what your body is telling you.

Maxi Pads: A Postpartum Mom's Tarot Cards

No one likes to wear maxi pads, let alone examine them in great detail, but when it comes to sex, it's a pretty clear-cut way to know when and whether sex is in your cards.

Regardless of whether you've graduated from the honkin' diaper-sized maxi pads back down to mini pads, if you're still bleeding, you're still healing, and you should not accept any visitors, invited or not, into your nethers. The six-week phase is a generous time period for ensuring that bleeding has completely stopped. (Most women will see it cease after about four weeks.)

A key to knowing if your body is physically ready for sex is to examine your activity level as it relates to the leakage. If you increase your physical activity to stair climbs or daily walks and you are forced back into the big pads, then you need to take it easy and put a hold on sex.

If there was ever a time to listen to your body, this would be it. Consider your pads the crystal ball of your sexual future. Anything but a fairly clean slate means that sex is not meant to be, at least until you do the next reading.

Haven't Got Time for the Pain

Along with keeping an eagle eye on your underpants, you'll want to make sure you've totally retired the ice-pack diapers and Percocets before doing the deed. Your level of pain will be directly related to tearing or episiotomy, and the subsequent stitching required.

MOMINATRIX SAYS

Tylenol is listed as a safe medication for pregnant and breast-feeding mothers. But it's always best to consult your physician before taking anything.

There's a long-standing argument as to whether it's better to tear or be cut, both of which probably give you an incredibly unpleasant tingle down below. Neither offer any great options; tearing is usually more superficial, but stitching it up can be difficult since it's uneven. An episiotomy usually gets the demon rap, but it can often be easier to stitch since it's a clean incision, purposely made by a doctor.

Of course, if you actually had an option you'd definitely prefer neither, so make sure to do perineum massage, and talk with your doctor or midwife later in your pregnancy to establish your preference. Look, no woman wants to tear or be cut down there, but if it's a matter of getting the baby out safely, then you'd probably let them cut off your baby toe.

As bad as it sounds and can feel, your nether regions heal pretty quickly, particularly compared to a c-section incision, which requires staples, butterfly Band-Aids, and a decent amount of attention and care.

When you're able to stand, sit, and complete all bodily functions without pain, that's a good sign that you're probably ready for intercourse. But know that it can take a while before you feel completely comfortable during sex, particularly in positions that offer you deeper penetration.

MOMINATRIX SAYS

If you're still feeling pain during sex after a couple of months, talk to your doctor or midwife. It might take a bit of time for you to readjust, but you shouldn't feel actual pain during intercourse. There might be some issues with your incision and subsequent mending that still require some attention.

Is Your Head in the Game?

Once you're confident that your body is on the mend, take two seconds and imagine yourself having sex. If the thought of you and your partner humping like rabbits with breastmilk leaking and loose skin flapping around is actually appealing and not stomach turning, then you just might be ready. But if you can barely go near your vagina, let alone think about putting anything inside it, then you might just want to think twice. Of course, those feelings can certainly change in an instant, since your emotions are riding a pretty crazy roller coaster ride, so make sure to take a few seconds—you know, in your free time—to check in with how you're feeling about sex.

Depending on how things are going with your recovery and your new role as a mom, you might be surprised at how quickly your sexual appetite returns. Many women report being turned on by watching their partners care for their babies. Have him do a little vacuuming and cooking, and you might get downright horny. Granted, a series of diaper changes and laundry loads might not seem like the greatest aphrodisiac, particularly if you and your partner had an enviable sex life prior to having kids. But like the other bazillion things that change when a baby arrives, so does your idea of foreplay.

If you do find yourself getting turned on, even with the sleep deprivation and the sore boobs, then you might just be ready to hop back into the sack. Any spark amidst what can be an incredibly exhausting and trying time is always a good sign. Of course, finding the opportunity to capitalize on it might be an entirely different story, but it's best to tackle one battle at a time.

Keep in mind that postpartum sexual signals can be extremely difficult to read, mostly due to the lack of lubrication that occurs courtesy of hormones that are producing your breastmilk and shrinking your uterus. And if you're breastfeeding, your nipples might be too sore, tired, and otherwise preoccupied to help send the message they're usually so effective at getting across. So whereas you might have typically gotten wet at the thought of your partner ravaging you over the bathroom sink, these days you might just get a little tingle, if that.

MOMINATRIX SAYS

Women find that breastfeeding can actually provide a satisfying sensation, at least once you get past the first two weeks of Nipple Boot Camp. You're not a freak for getting off when your tiny baby sucks on your nipples. It's a completely autonomic physical response and no reason for anyone to call protective services on you.

The emotional roller coaster that is the first few weeks and even months of motherhood can also cause a bit of static interference, so just do your best to check in with yourself, even if it's only for the couple of minutes while you try to use the bathroom alone.

These changes do not mean, however, that you shouldn't try to get it on. With a bit of outside assistance, you'll feel your libido kicking into drive, and before you know it, you'll be on autopilot in no time.

THE POSTPARTUM BODY

Picturing yourself in the throngs of hot, wild sex becomes a bit more complicated when you factor in that bedraggled postpartum body. Regardless of how much weight you gained and subsequently lost when you had the baby, the six-week time period (or less, if you're particularly spritely) doesn't necessarily allow for full body recovery. Basically, while your vagina might be ready for playtime, your other parts might still need a little assistance before they feel somewhat normal.

Depending on the length and intensity of your labor, you could be walking around on a set of exhausted legs. And you'll be surprised at how sore your back and arms can get after carrying that little baby around for more hours than you probably thought possible. Instead of constantly reminding yourself about your pre-baby body, save your sanity by adjusting your definition of "normal" from what your body used to be like before the baby to its current state.

It took you a good solid ten months to gain all the baby weight, so you shouldn't expect it to just fall off in a couple of weeks. Most women do not fit back into their pre-baby clothes immediately postpartum (surprise!), so instead of continually disappointing yourself by trying to squeeze back into them, put them away for a good solid few months, or at least until your early or mid-maternity clothes are loose, which could be longer than you think.

Courtesy of a tiny baby resting within your pelvis for more than nine months, your organs, ligaments, and bones will have to adjust back to their regular positions, and unlike the extra water fluids and fat that you can attempt to lose, it's a bit more difficult to move your intestines back into place. So while you might have lost the actual baby weight and a bunch more thanks to all those fluids, your out-of-whack body can be terribly hard to fit into clothes that are made based on typical proportions. And there's just nothing typical about breasts that change sizes almost daily, a waist that has been stretched like a cheap elastic band that doesn't pop back, and hips that have spread so a baby could travel through. Until someone invents an actual postpartum mom sizing system, you're stuck with every new mom's staple outfit: stretch pants and big T-shirts.

Nursing Bras Have Come a Long Way, Baby

If you do find a few choice articles of clothing that fit, you can't really have sex with all of them on — no matter how well they work to disguise a flabby belly, engorged breasts, and stretch marks. But fear not, there are plenty of options for moms who might be ready to get it on but can't seem to bring themselves to romp around in their birthday suits. Thankfully, nursing bras and underwear are no longer made to look like they should be hidden under ugly shirts and elastic-waisted pants. Granted, you can still purchase some pretty scary bras, but thanks to companies that have learned that just because you've got a baby sucking on your boobs doesn't mean you don't necessarily want your husband to have a turn, you can sift through the fugly crap and find a slew of functional, sexy breastfeeding intimates. A lacy nursing bra may offer you a bit of normalcy — at least until you have to hike up your shirt, pop it open, and stick your baby on your boob again.

MOMINATRIX SAYS

The breastfeeding police might scold you for using underwire, but the truth is, you probably need it to hold up those big milky jugs. Just make sure you're wearing the correct size, and don't sleep in your underwire bras.

That being said, these intimate moments might be a great time to give that nursing bra — lacy or not — a short break. After all, you're probably not going to have to stop mid-sex to go feed the baby, and if you do, you can just take your bra completely off to do so. It's hard to remember that nursing bras were created as a convenience and are not completely essential to the breastfeeding experience.

If a sexy nursing bra doesn't seem that practical or appealing, hop over to your local popular lingerie joint and grab a couple of sexy bras and panties. Just make sure to get sized. While you might not want them to measure your waist, you may be pleasantly surprised at your new and vastly improved bra size.

THE MOMINATRIX'S TOP THREE FAVORITE NURSING BRAS		
Condessa	www.condessainc.com	You won't break your budget with these nursing bra and panty sets, and you might actually wear them after the baby is weaned. Who said popping out a boob meant taking off your entire bra. You might as well use the nursing hooks to your advantage.
Agent Provocateur	www.agentprovocateur.com	A celebrity fave for folks with celebrity-sized wallets, these gorgeous, nearly handcrafted sets are definitely worth all the hype. Just make sure you don't decide to *rip* them off during hot sex; you'll probably spend a solid month paying for them.
Bella Materna	www.bellamaterna.com	The French Lace Maternity Collection was created with the large-breasted woman in mind. They'll keep your breasts up where they belong without making you feel like you're wearing some sort of 1950s straitjacket.

Corsets 2.0

Your floppy belly can be easily contained with the assistance of a nursing tank, or any regular old tank top, for that matter. But if you've been living in them for the last few months, it might be a nice change of scenery for yourself and your partner if you try wearing something a bit more provocative.

And no, that doesn't mean wearing a lacy nursing tank.

Consider spicing things up with a sexy body-slimming tank or a corset of some kind. It will keep everything contained and intact during "the wild ride," and if you've got an adjustable one, it might even shrink you down a couple of sizes. Plus they have a tendency to push your boobs together and up—a position that's flattering for all breasts, regardless of shape and size.

Just be sure you don't squeeze the tank or corset so hard that you can't breathe, even if the color blue is thinning. And while you're not going to be wearing these every day, if you do have a place to go other than the mailbox, or if you are returning to work, you'll definitely get more than just the bedroom use of the slimmer or corset.

And remember: When all else fails, pure darkness and a few drinks can remedy almost any pregnancy-induced bodily imperfection.

MOMINATRIX SAYS

Small amounts of alcohol and caffeine have been found safe for breastfeeding mothers. Use your discretion and consult your doctor with any questions or concerns.

SEX ISN'T JUST ABOUT INTERCOURSE

If the thought of intercourse still makes you run for the hills, that's not to say you don't have any other options. In fact, it's not such a bad idea to ease yourself back into the saddle instead of jumping on bareback, especially when day and night are running together and you haven't left your house for a week or two. And if your partner is a bit nervous about getting back in the saddle again, he'll be more than happy to engage in a little "pre-game warm-up" right along with you; no bribing necessary. Given your current schedule, you probably don't have the stamina to engage in full-on sex for longer than a couple of minutes, if that. And while that might be a long time for your husband, you'll want to give yourself ample time for your first journey back. You'll need a few minutes to get the bed set up, let alone actually do it in that amount of time.

Finding the time to separate yourself from your offspring might be challenging, but if you want to re-womanize yourself, consider engaging in some good old-fashioned fooling around instead of spending those precious minutes trying to squeeze yourself into your old pants.

Foreplay

While the "running of the bases" is decidedly high school—or middle school for you bad girls—the nostalgia might just be enough to make you feel less like a breeder and more like a woman again. And considering you'd rather take a few quiet minutes or hours to stare at the insides of your eyelids, some simple petting and making out can provide you with stimulation without a big-time investment or mess to clean up.

Sex Games

While you might giggle and roll your eyes at the thought of playing sexual board or card games, they don't sell them because no one buys them. They're popular because you can add a little humor into your sex life, which is something most postpartum moms could definitely use more of. You'll find everything from sex dice to playing cards to board games complete with game pieces and tokens, all of which can be a fun way to ease yourself back into the real game. And if you're still feeling goofy, add some wine into the mix. Since your tolerance has probably dropped down to nothing due to ten months of forced sobriety, you'll really only need a glass to ease your nerves.

MOMINATRIX SAYS

You can actually play a good old-fashioned sex game with a pair of dice. Just decide which numbers correspond with what sexual acts and shoot away. If you're a bit more competitive or just want more help than a couple of dice can offer, try the Nookii game (*www.nookii.com*). It definitely reinvents the term "game night."

Mutual Masturbation

If a good old-fashioned hand job makes you feel like some high school bad girl (or worse, a cheap prostitute), you're not alone. But add in a little mutually beneficial hand stimulation and it's not that bad. And what's great is that while you might not have had sex on the brain, an effective session of mutual hand stimulation might even warm you up enough for the real thing. And if it doesn't, it can still get the job done quite effectively all on its very own.

Giving Oral Sex

If you enjoy the spirit of giving, then there's nothing wrong with offering to provide your partner with a bit of oral pleasure—when it's under your own terms, of course. You're already spending the day caring for each and every need of a little person, so the idea of caring for someone's penis might not be as appealing as it used to be. If your partner is willing to give you oral sex, and you feel comfortable enough letting him dive down into what might be a very scary place, then it's totally your call. Just keep the baby wipes close by. And the mouthwash.

Sex Toys

If you tend to keep your sex toys locked in your nightstand drawer, bring them out in the light of day—or night—and use them together with your partner. And depending on the toy, you might even be able to enjoy the stimulation while fully dressed. Plus there's really nothing else that can provide a successful and quite timely experience than a damn good sex toy. If you want a few suggestions for parent-friendly sex toys (you know, toys that look a bit more discrete in case your kids find them), check out Chapter 8.

GETTING DOWN TO BUSINESS

The worst thing you can probably do when you decide that you're ready to have sex again is to hype it up to be a big event. Unless you've waited until your kids are school-age to do it, you're dealing with a terribly short window of time, none of which should be used to toss rose petals on the bed or light three hundred candles. One sneeze and you could wake up the baby and set your room on fire.

You're not losing your virginity at some post-prom party so you shouldn't treat it as such. It might seem romantic to act like it's this super-duper-huge life-changing event, but it's just sex, plain and simple. You did it before, obviously, and you'll definitely be doing it again. And unfortunately, you probably won't have the time or energy to do anything but get your clothes off and flop on the bed, let alone set the mood.

Pre-Game Considerations

It's incredibly important to realize that biology is working against you right now. Basically, your hormones are on crack, and in order for you to feed your child, your body is suppressing your progesterone levels. Any and all fluids you might have had are either being sucked out of you by your tiny baby or leaking into your terribly sexy nursing bra. Also, the only wetness you are feeling is when you accidentally piss yourself because you never did those Kegels.

MOMINATRIX SAYS

Even if you didn't do Kegels once during your pregnancy, skip over to Chapter 4 and start doing them now. Right now. They can firm everything up, make your orgasms stronger, and keep you from peeing yourself. Wearing Depends is the antithesis of sexy.

And to top things off, if your baby is a boy, you're already dealing with a penis and balls way more than should be humanly allowed. Aside from having to tuck it down in a diaper and wipe it clean about fifteen times a day, you're dodging what tends to be more like a renegade hose. So don't be surprised if seeing a daddy-sized hard one waving in your face after is not the biggest turn-on. Any mystery that might have been stuffed down in your husband's pants is now gone courtesy of your son's diaper.

But whatever the gender of your baby, you're probably dealing with conflicting emotions: a new type of love that you've never felt before and a transition between roles for both you and your partner. Having a baby can be the singularly most amazing and gut-wrenchingly difficult life event, and there's just no escaping what that can do to your own psyche as well as your relationship. That's why you've got to make sure that you and your partner have realistic expectations on what's about to go down.

Finally Doing the Deed

If you've gotten some rest and feel a tinge of sexual desire, take it slow and make sure your partner understands that concept: *go slow*. Be resigned to the fact that not only will you need lots of lube but there's also a good chance your boobs will leak. So living-room-couch sex is probably not in the cards. And while you won't have a ton of time to smother the bedroom in romance, do what you can to set some sort of sex mood. That could involve anything from changing the sheets and your underpants, to just removing all the breast pads and burp cloths from your bed. And it might mean preemptively turning off all the lights and slugging a couple of glasses of Merlot; daylight does not do a floppy postpartum belly and engorged breastfeeding boobs any justice. There's no shame in demanding complete darkness and drunkenness. In fact, you might find a fuzzy pitch-black room to be a turn-on.

Most important, nothing kills an erection quicker than a screaming baby, so don't feel bad or disappointed if your lovemaking is interrupted by your new bundle of joy. It's bound to happen, so preparing yourself in advance will help you avoid any disappointment.

If at First You Don't Succeed

There's a good chance that your first time back might be terribly anticlimactic. Literally. So don't waste any more minutes worrying about what you're going to do and how it's going to be. Try your best to just turn off your brain and rid yourselves of all the weird nerves and ridiculous expectations so you'll actually enjoy it the next time you try. And since you and your body have changed since the last time you went at it, you and your partner might require a reorientation session before things actually work the way they used to. Parts may have shifted in the move, so you might need a little bit of time to figure out where things are and how they work again.

It's super-important to communicate what works and what doesn't so that your partner can help relearn your body with you. It's sort of like exploring new territory without a map or fancy GPS system; he can waste time by driving around in circles or do the smart thing and stop to ask for directions. But considering how long it takes a dude to pull over, don't wait until he asks. Let him know that he's headed in the wrong direction before he gets lost.

MOMINATRIX SAYS

For the first few times back, choose positions that give you control over the penetration. This way you can ease yourself back into it at your own pace. Pain tends to kill the mood pretty quickly.

If you find that things aren't working the way that you remember, even after a few tries, that doesn't mean all bets are off. Don't be discouraged or throw in the towel. Whether you do it every night or once a month, you've got to make it a priority to keep trying once you pop your postpartum cherry. At some point, you'll learn to ignore the crying baby, deal with the floppy belly, and enjoy yourself.

Every sexual relationship can use an overhaul to keep things exciting. So see this challenge as an opportunity to pull yourself out of that missionary-position rut you might have been in before you got knocked up. Plus, if you're able to approach things with an open mind and fairly low expectations, you'll have less chance of being disappointed. Celebrate that you were able to carve out the time to actually try to have sex instead of moping about not being able to reach a climax. Sure, postpartum sex might be just like riding a bike, but only if your bike's seat got moved around and one of the pedals needs some extra elbow grease to get it to turn.

So grab your big blank playbook and fill it up with all sorts of new tricks.

But whatever you do, for God's sake use a condom.

3

ADJUSTING
TO BABY

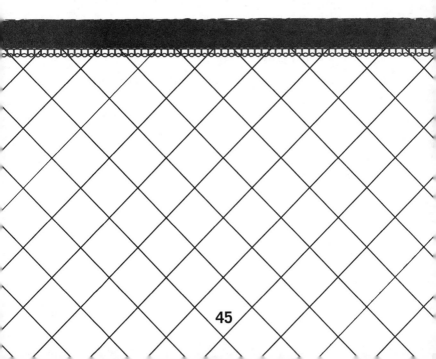

So the good news is that physically you're ready to hop back in the saddle again for regular rides. But the bad news is that you've just had a baby, and actually finding a small—even two-minute—window when the stars are perfectly aligned to give you an opportunity to do the deed before you're interrupted by your new precious bundle is a whole other story.

And that's not taking into account any of the challenges new moms tend to face when dealing with newborns. Add the diaper changes, endless feedings, and ridiculous amounts of laundry, and you're lucky that you can actually spell *sex*, let alone have it.

Regardless of whether you've gotten your groove back or you've scraped together some semblance of what used to be your libido out of desperation, you don't need to keep your roles of sexual woman and loving mother separate. While it might take longer than you'd like for the two personas to become one, jumping back in the sack again will certainly help you feel less like an apparition of your former self and more like an actual human being. In fact, it might be nice to get a little break from being somebody's mother. You're working way more than an eight-hour day, with no weekends off. Just don't be surprised if you need a bit of a map to get you to the *X* that marks your special spot.

Of course, if babies popped out with their own instructional manual, or at least one in your native tongue, perhaps the transition from kidless to kid-centered would be a bit easier. But unless you were Mother Teresa in another life and have the karma of a saint, chances are that you'll have to deal with one or more of the newborn issues that plague a new mom's ability to function at the basic human level, let alone act like a sexual being. Fortunately, most of those issues can be dealt with through a few minor adjustments to how you generally do your "business," which in the long scheme of things, especially considering how many adjustments you've already made, shouldn't be too big of a deal.

SLEEP

Clearly, the lack of sleep will instantly decapitate your libido, particularly one that's been through the hormonal ringer. No matter how angelic your baby is, you will still be on a whacked-out schedule that will require you to be awake way more often than you ever thought humanly possible. And unfortunately, there's very little you can do about it, especially in the first few months, except take every single annoying person's advice and sleep when the baby sleeps.

Now, actually making that happen might take some feat of nature, especially if you've got other wee ones running around. However it's incredibly important to get as much sleep as possible, not only for the sake of your sex life, but quite frankly, for your own sanity. Sleep deprivation can make you do crazy things, and considering you're already riding the wave of a pretty strong cocktail of postpartum hormones, you'll want to make an effort to sleep to stop you from totally going ape-shit. If you're breastfeeding, that might mean pumping so your partner can do one middle-of-the-night feeding, or even letting your partner give the baby one bottle of formula. Rest assured, Junior will not lose automatic admittance to an Ivy League school because you served the powdered crap. In fact, many smart and productive citizens were formula-fed.

If you're really struggling with a baby who's not so keen on the concept of sleep, you might consider letting the baby sleep with you. Now, a co-sleeping baby doesn't necessarily make your return to an active sexual relationship easier, but in some cases, it will help you get more sleep. And you can bet that a well-rested mom probably has a much better chance at wanting sex.

MOMINATRIX SAYS

If you plan on giving co-sleeping a whirl, make sure you're familiar with the safety issues involved. You'll find plenty of resources that will offer you quick tips on how to keep your co-sleeping experience a positive and healthy one.

Worried that a baby in your bed will put a damper on the activities? C'mon—live a little. You can always have sex somewhere other than your bed. But getting sleep on the floor, in your closet, or on the kitchen table is way less likely.

The sleep deprivation is pretty much unavoidable during the first few months, particularly if you're not sleeping when your baby sleeps or if you have a baby who doesn't like to sleep. Around the third or fourth month, you'll notice that the baby's awake and sleep time will become more consistent. This should allow you to get a good three- to four-hour stretch. If you're still not getting enough rest, you might want to grab a few books on the subject, or even hire a sleep consultant. Any money invested on getting your baby to sleep will be well worth it—not just for you but for your relationship in general. Life with a baby who hates to sleep can be miserable for everyone.

STRESS

On top of sleep deprivation, early motherhood, regardless of whether you're a rookie or a seasoned mom, can be pretty damn stressful. It'll make a crier out of you, much to your dismay, if not from the sheer weight of the responsibility then certainly from the good old hormones kicking your ass. And the lack of consistency and predictability, except that life will be consistently unpredictable, makes life with babies inordinately more complicated, preparation or not.

Surprise! A stressed-out mom generally wants nothing to do with sex.

Regardless of what everyone has told you about where the baby should sleep or when the baby should eat, you sometimes just have to toss out all the parenting books and do what works for you and your family. It can be difficult to learn to trust your gut and not rely on the expert advice of "Dr. So-and-So," but remember that this doctor has never met you *or* your baby and therefore may not have the cure-all to rid your challenging little monster of this aversion to sleep. Granted, the expert may have thought of something that your poor tired brain has not and, on the flip side, might even reassure you about the decisions that you thought were completely off the wall.

But even if this is your first baby and you're worried that the kid will need years of therapy if you allow sleeping in the baby swing or sucking for long periods of time on a pacifier, know that in the extremely long span of your child's life, Junior will not be emotionally damaged because you permitted sleeping in a moving object while sucking on a piece of nipple-shaped plastic. The truth is that Junior will be more damaged if you don't take care of yourself.

One quick scan of the parenting section at your local bookstore will reap an overwhelming number of parenting "methods"—some of which might offer fantastic insight into your kids and others that aren't worth their weight in snot. That doesn't mean you have to go "balls to the walls" and follow one method like some devout cult member. Pick and choose what works for you. It's great if it works for your kid, but if it's killing you, then it can actually breed resentment. And it's important that you like your kid, at least until the teenage years.

Decide what you feel you can sacrifice, such as the Baby Mandarin lessons, and then figure out your deal breakers: those principles and values that you just don't feel your child can live without. Maybe that means you forgo the homemade organic baby food for the jarred stuff, or you get a babysitter a few times a week instead of spending every single waking hour with your baby. Your kids will be fine, and you might even be a better mom for it, thanks to the extra time in your day to actually breathe. And *please* don't compare yourself to any other mom, including your own. They're not parenting your kids, and you shouldn't let what they do with their own families impact what you do with yours, unless they've got some magical way to get your baby to stop crying and sleep soundly.

Tending to the basic needs of another human being is a huge responsibility that will challenge even the most capable person. Managing the simple everyday requirements such as feeding, changing, and comforting can be pretty overwhelming, so don't be surprised if you find yourself melting into one big puddle of tears and baby poop. But then you should probably expect your libido to melt right along with you.

FEEDING

Before you start defending your feeding choices, realize that whatever method you're using—exclusively breast-feeding, pumping, or formula—should not cause you any sense of guilt. You'll do enough other things that will warrant way more guilt, so just save it for the times you do something that you need to feel bad about.

Granted, if you are formula feeding, you've got one less excuse for skipping sex because your boobs, aside from the first couple of weeks when your milk is drying up, should be good to go. Breastfeeding moms may find a few more challenges to getting it on. In the early weeks, you might end up with a bit of scabbing on your nipples and a lot of swelling on your breasts, particularly as your baby figures out the latch and your milk supply evens out. With your breasts feeling like big sore rocks, you might be in a completely "hands off unless you're a tiny screaming baby" situation when it comes to your precious peaches. And with your breasts decidedly off limits, you might find yourself less than motivated to do anything that remotely involves sex with your partner, especially if they are a regular part of your sexual routine.

Once your baby gets the hang of it, the only issue is the leaking, which really just makes sex a bit messier. But, since you've probably already got a towel down or at least in close quarters, just go for it. The smell of breastmilk mixed with sweat is actually pretty sweet. And the extra bit of leakage might save you from having to pump later on, or deal with engorged boobs in the middle of the night.

MOMINATRIX SAYS

Stuff your bra with a couple of breast pads and have sex with it on. It might take some adjustment, particularly if you enjoyed having your breasts stimulated by your partner, but it's doable. And you won't have to worry about squirting him in the eyeball with breastmilk.

COLIC

There's nothing like a constantly screaming baby to send your sanity and your libido packing for a solid six months. And frankly, even a mildly fussy baby can be difficult to deal with—even more so if the fussing happens at the exact moment you're trying to get it on. Babies have amazing timing like that. And while you might be able to have sex through earthquakes, tornadoes, and other acts of God, doing it while a baby screams in the room next to you might just land you on *Ripley's Believe It or Not!*

Colic is caused by any number of things. And when you think about it, it sort of makes sense, since the baby was tucked sweetly in your belly for the last nine months and is now out in the big wide world. No more comforting warm belly no more reassuring heartbeat nearby. You'd probably be pissed off too.

But true fussy-baby colic is most often attributed to gas, reflux, allergies, and/or overall discomfort that might actually be treatable, so it will behoove you to talk to your pediatrician if you get the sense that your baby has colic. On the bright side, that won't be too difficult to determine. There are several remedies—everything from change of diet to medication—that could make a huge difference.

BABY BLUES

Most postpartum moms experience some type of hormonal dip, oftentimes called "Baby Blues." That can include anything from crying at the drop of the hat to biting off your partner's head because he looked at you the wrong way. Be prepared to experience this in one way or another, so keep a box of tissues nearby and warn your partner in advance.

Mothering is a hard job on its own, but the hormones can seriously confound the situation. And it can continue throughout the first year of your baby's life, especially if you're breastfeeding. Think PMS times 10.

Sleep can certainly help to brighten your mood, and making efforts to return to your general state of being—assuming you can remember what that was—will also help. That means taking a long shower, doing your hair and putting on makeup, or letting someone take the baby for a good solid hour so you can check your e-mail. If that doesn't do it, get out and go shopping, even if it's only for a few minutes. New clothes that have yet to see spit-up stains and poop smudges, even if they are a few sizes above what you'd like to be, might just be a way to help dig out from the postpartum funk.

The early weeks of motherhood can be terribly dehumanizing, so allowing yourself to enjoy typical human activities that don't necessarily involve your baby, even if it is for just a few minutes, can be a good way to turn your baby blues a lighter shade. Even an uninterrupted cup of coffee or a solo potty break can bring a smile to a new mom's face.

MOMINATRIX SAYS

Keep your expectations for each day low. If you fed the baby, changed a couple of diapers, and remembered to feed yourself, you did really well. Anything else you can do is just icing on the cake.

Let's say you've made it through all the trials and tribulations that are oftentimes just par for the course with a new baby. This has probably left you with a whopping 2.7 minutes of actual free time, most of which you'd probably rather use for eating an actual warm meal or sleeping. But since hot food and a catnap don't have the potential to give you the level of satisfaction that sex could offer, you've made the right choice.

SEX IT IS!

Now whether or not 2.7 minutes covers how long your previous sexual encounters lasted, you'll definitely need to make some adjustments to make sex work. Thankfully, none really require any monetary investment. Instead, they require you to be a bit more creative than you might initially feel you have the energy for. But the thought of an orgasm should be enough to get your adrenaline pumping. And chances are, you'll need it.

MOMINATRIX **SAYS**

If you do find yourself crying a lot, or feeling like you want to hurt yourself or the baby, then tell someone immediately. Postpartum depression, at any level, can be paralyzing and should be treated by a health professional.

Make a Sex Appointment

Scheduling sex is most definitely not for everyone. However, you'd be surprised at how effective it can actually be. Since babies tend to do things on their own schedule, you might find that making the appointment is a bit easier than actually keeping it.

Creating a schedule might just add some much needed consistency to your life. Yes, there will be consistency. Say it over and over again. Of course it might be consistently chaotic, but still, even that is predictable.

So making a point to have sex on a specific day or night can actually be hot in that it will give you the chance to prepare for the appointment with an extra-long, five-minute shower and lower-leg shave. But even better, you can ensure that your baby will be occupied, hopefully by sleeping soundly, when it occurs.

MOMINATRIX SAYS

If the idea of scheduled sex bores you, then have some fun with it. Knowing in advance simply allows you to prepare more. Light a few candles and pop on a pair of unmatronly panties for the big morning or night.

Of course, as Murphy's Parental Law would have it, expect your infant to decide to go through a sleep regression on your scheduled sex day, so be prepared for interruptions. Set aside a fairly long window of time, not necessarily because you're going to go at it for a solid hour, but rather so you won't be disappointed if you've got to tend to the baby a few times. And don't worry if you have to reschedule. The idea that you're taking the effort to actually have sex is a good start. At some point in time, the sleep gods will shine favorably upon you and you'll eventually get laid.

Time of Day

Thanks to new motherhood, you're probably on a twenty-four-hour-a-day schedule. Most likely, your days and nights are running together to a point where, aside from the darkness, the only way you know it's night is that you're watching bad movie reruns and infomercials with the sound of your snoring partner in the background.

So try to look on the bright side (literally) by using your new schedule to your advantage. In other words, have sex at a different time of day. For moms who are decidedly night rompers, the transition from night to day can be challenging and uncomfortable. The idea of having sex under the bright light of the morning or afternoon sun is probably not the most ideal situation for a new mom who would much rather hide the floppy post-baby belly in pitch darkness. But when you think about it, you'll be somewhat alert and awake, even if it is after your fourth cup of coffee. Attempting to get it on at the end of a very long day might not necessarily be the best choice for you or your partner, particularly if you need more than a two-minute romp in the sheets.

This doesn't necessarily mean you have to do it with the blinds open and the curtains drawn back. Figure out a way to get your room dark, perhaps by installing sun-blocking window shades which can double in your baby's room. Or you can play MacGyver and take the extremely effective aluminum foil route. Granted it might not be as dark as you'd like, and Martha Stewart would probably have a heart attack, but it's way better than watching the sunlight reflect off your ass. And if you've got a baby with a fairly consistent daytime schedule, then you'll know exactly how long you have before feeding time.

If you suck it up (and in), day sex is definitely worth a try. Not only will both of you be fresher, but since many babies have more consistent daytime schedules, you might actually be able to hit it without interruptions. And then you can save bedtime for what it's intended—lying around waiting for your baby to wake up.

Quiet Sex

One thing that happens to every single new parent is that you become obsessed with keeping the baby asleep. You stick the "Don't ring the doorbell or be castrated" sign out for the mailman, you know which door makes the loud creaky noise that shall not be touched during specific times of the day, and your voices drop at least ten full decibels. So when it comes to sex, you'll most definitely want to put a plug in it (your mouth, silly), because there's just no other way to kill the mood like waking up a perfectly sleeping baby.

However, regardless of how determined you are to keep that baby asleep, don't make some sworn pact of silent sex. You're trying to actually enjoy it, and for the most part, a well-timed groan, grunt, or "Oh God" can actually enhance the experience. Just make sure to use your now well-mastered "inside" voice or soft whisper when you're doing it, since you don't want your kid's first words to be "It's soooo big."

If you're worried that you won't be able to keep your enjoyment to a soft roar, steal your baby's white noise machine, or get one for yourself. It's a fantastic way to block out any ambient noise, and it also helps to keep out any stray yelps or gasps that might come from your direction during sex. And now might be the time to reignite the use of music in the bedroom, not only as a means to cover your hot slapping bodies, but also as a way to get you back in the mood.

MOMINATRIX SAYS

Download your fave sex songs to your iPod and consider investing in a small stereo system for your bedroom. It won't take up any space and it'll give you some background noise without a huge investment.

The Mominatrix's Sex Playlist

Make Another Baby Songs
- **Van Morrison:** "Crazy Love"
- **Ray LaMontagne:** "Hold You in My Arms"
- **James Blunt:** "Beautiful"
- **Lauryn Hill:** "You're Just Too Good to Be True"
- **Mazzy Star:** "Fade into You"
- **Dave Matthews Band:** "Crash"
- **Coldplay:** "In My Place"

Bang Me 'til Tomorrow Songs
- **Madonna:** "Justify My Love" (or the entire *Erotica* album)
- **Isley Brothers:** "Between the Sheets"
- **Fiona Apple:** "Criminal"
- **Timbaland and Nelly Furtado:** "Promiscuous Girl"
- **AC/DC:** "You Shook Me All Night Long"
- **Keith Sweat:** "Twisted"

Love in an Elevator

It's no secret that bedtime in general causes anxiety in many parents, particularly if you've got a child who thinks sleep is not a requirement for survival. You can barely lay your head down to sleep let alone have any type of hot sex without jerking up at any small squawk or cry.

And if you've got a baby who sleeps with you, sex in your bed will be nearly impossible. Nothing says instant turnoff like looking over at your sweetly sleeping baby while your husband is banging you with your legs high in the air. I think that might even dry Jenna Jameson right up.

To be clear, this is not to suggest jumping on the nearest park bench and scrumping like monkeys in front of half the neighborhood. While you might be able to get a better night's sleep in the slammer, there are probably only a few people who can sit comfortably on a park bench, let alone screw on one.

But instead of making the bed your sexual meeting place, look around your house and figure out what might be a titillating place to get it on. It can also be a great excuse for making the housecleaning a bit more enjoyable. Stake out the good spots and make certain your partner won't be eating Goldfish cracker crumbs out of your pubic hair later that evening.

The Mominatrix's Top Five Great Bed Alternatives

1. *The floor.* Your carpet or strategically covered hardwood has no weight or size restriction. And you've got lots of room to move around.
2. *The kitchen.* Receiving oral with your ass on the counter can be quite memorable. Just make sure the stove is off.
3. *The shower.* Turn off the water after a while. No need to catch a cold or, worse, a chafed vagina.
4. *Over the bathroom sink.* The mirror can be your friend. If not, breathe hard.
5. *The walk-in closet.* Dark, enclosed small spaces can be very hot. Just make sure to move the shoes or, better, wear them.

In most cases, you'll be able to rekindle your sex life with an open mind and a few minor adjustments to your regular routine. Plus, since any semblance of your pre-kid routine has already gone completely out the window, it shouldn't be that hard to make changes.

WHEN HE'S JUST NOT THAT INTO IT

Sometimes the simple change in scenery or schedule might not be enough, particularly if your desire to have sex shot out with your placenta. It's not uncommon to suffer from PPSD (Post-Partum Sex Disorder), a completely unscientific and unprofessional diagnosis that affects more women than you'd probably guess. Usually, however, once you're able to get a handle on all the changes that have just occurred, you'll find that your sex drive returns over the course of a few months. Keep in mind that if you are breastfeeding, you may continue to experience a low sex drive until you begin to wean and/or your feeding schedule becomes less vigorous. It has little to do with the physical requirements involved with breastfeeding and more to do with those lovely hormones that inhibit your moisture production.

If you find that your sex drive has ramped up after having a baby, regardless of how many sleepless nights you've had, you might be unpleasantly surprised when your husband happens to be the one suffering from PPSD. New moms can actually use the headache excuse and mean it, thanks to the loud, squawking baby. However, the idea that new dads aren't interested in sex is not talked about as often, most likely due to society's gender stereotypes that create the image of a crazed, sex-hungry dad laying his hard penis on his sleeping partner's thigh every night.

So when Daddy is not interested in sex, particularly if his libido was alive and kicking before the kid arrived, it can be quite startling.

It's especially difficult to accept a husband with PPSD, because sexual interest tends to help the poor, exhausted new mom's self-esteem, which is probably a bit low, particularly if you're still sporting your maternity pants and trudging around in a big ugly nursing bra. If there's anything that could perk up a mom, it's a well-executed romantic seduction that is completely devoid of ass smacks and boob grabs. Just a good old-fashioned "Damn, I want to make love to you" usually does the trick.

Of course, if you haven't had any type of sexual contact in a really long time, you might be happy for a middle-of-the-night poke. But if your husband has PPSD, any such smack, grab, or poke is clearly an accident, thus leaving you feeling less attractive than you already do.

There's a good chance that you're not the root cause of your partner's sudden loss of libido, but if you're still concerned, take a few seconds to answer these questions:

Do you require large farm equipment to remove you from a bed?

Do you have a disfiguring and rancid case of genital herpes?

Have you threatened your partner with dangerous kitchen utensils so that he should fear for his life?

Noes across the board, right? *Good.*

Chances are it has absolutely nothing to do with you. The research, should you care about that, shows that most men who are cheating show *hypersexual* behavior, so you can probably rule that one out. And while stress and sleep deprivation can certainly affect sexual desire and performance, if you're up for it after your long days as a mother (working outside of the home or not), then long days at the job that do not involve diapers is no excuse for him. So, let's look at a few other possibilities:

He's all used up from all those dirty whores in college. Not so far off considering men hit their sexual prime at around seventeen.

He's old and crusty. Well, so is Hugh Hefner, who doesn't seem to have a problem (if you take the three hot blondes and the Viagra into consideration).

He's gay. Quick quiz will answer that: does he religiously watch *The Real World*; does he know that Jimmy Choo is a shoe designer and not a Chinese chef; and, the kicker, does he perk up when you offer to wear a beard and let him stick you in the ass?

But really, chances are he's been sucked in by the sexed-out housewife club and thinks he's doing you a favor by letting you sleep, when really he might just need to know it's a priority for you. Of course, it seems odd that he could miss the message his naked partner is sending by trying to grab his dick, but perhaps you need to take a different approach: A conversation? A lengthy discussion? An e-mail? Regardless of how awkward you might feel trying to discuss the lack of what's going on in your bedroom, it can't be any worse than what you both endured having a baby. Remember, the guy saw a baby exhumed from your belly or, more likely, your crotch. Talking about the distressingly low or nonexistent levels of sex in your lives should be a cinch. And who knows, that might actually be the reason he's slow to recover. If you were brave enough to request a mirror during the end of your delivery, you shouldn't be surprised if he's looking at you a bit differently. It's heroic, for sure, but it's also a little disconcerting to see a baby pop out of "the happy place."

In that vein, there's definitely a bit of weight to the notion that he might be having trouble seeing you as a sexual being since you became a mother. Blame society instead of yourself for perpetuating the idea that mothers are highly undesirable unless they're sporting no visible evidence that they ever had children. Generally speaking, most definitions of a MILF don't include a mom running around in a dirty ponytail and stretched-out yoga pants with a couple of rugrats nipping at her ankles.

Lame as it might seem, it could just be that he's having a hard time adjusting to the new you—whether you're basically the same with just a few extra pounds on your waist and butt, or you've done a complete 180 and are hardly recognizable. And if you're having trouble blending mom, woman, and partner, then you might be having trouble with the adjustment yourself.

Carving out time for yourself to enjoy any semblance of your former existence can actually help rekindle the fire between you and your partner. Whether that means taking longer than usual to soak in the bathtub, or sneaking away for an hour and getting a pedicure, you'll start to feel more like your old self again, and chances are it will rub off on your partner as well.

Also, it's really important for you to find time together that doesn't involve the baby. This will help both of you to balance out your new roles. A simple meal that is specifically yours and has absolutely nothing to do with the baby—not even one mention of Junior—can often do wonders.

Of course, you've got to find time to do all this while taking care of a kid, which is sort of what got you into this situation in the first place. So long as you're discussing it openly with your partner and making combined efforts to make it work, then you'll discover that libidos should find their way back to working order in no time.

And if not, well, then there's always porn.

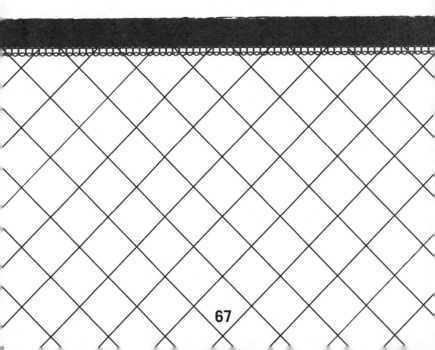

4

ADDRESSING
THE STATE OF
YOUR VAGINA

Regardless of whether or not you are a "squat on a mirror and peek" kind of girl, it's extremely important to reacquaint yourself with your special "lady" as part of your sexual reawakening, particularly if you had a baby or two pass through on their way into the world. Aside from hormones and just plain old age, the process of pushing out a baby through what is a fairly small opening can wreak havoc on what may now be less of a beautiful flower and more of a mutated plant. So if your orchid now resembles more of a Venus Fly Trap, you'll want to be completely aware of the hostile takeover.

Thankfully, the vagina is not known for its dashing good looks and won't be winning any beauty contests. But since she's been run through the ringer and lost her girlish charm, it's a good thing for you, as her owner and keeper, to know exactly what is going on down there. And unless you have a fliptop head or are a gold medal gymnast, you're going to have to do the whole leg-up-and-mirror thing. Depending on what came out of there, your little handheld makeup mirror is not going to cut it. In fact, you might want to choose the larger one you wanted to use during labor but then adamantly refused to because you realized that no sane person would want to see that. It's one thing to feel it, and a whole other one to watch it all go down.

So just be prepared for the first viewing of your postpartum nether regions. Even you moms with the strongest of stomachs might want to hold onto something before taking a look. Regardless of whether a baby passed through there or you had Junior pulled from your belly, most women's vaginas are swollen and extremely sensitive after having a baby. Add some stitches and lochia, and you're looking at one very scary sight.

FRANKENGINA: IT'S ALIVE! IT'S ALIVE!

Perhaps it wouldn't surprise you that women seem to know more about penises and testicles than they do about their own body parts. Women tend to be a gender of givers, after all. Many women are well acquainted with the fourteen pleasure points on the shaft of a penis and head, but they can be directionally challenged when it comes to finding their clitoris and clueless to what exactly constitutes a vulva. So aside from the fact that you might not recognize your vagina, it's probable that you might not know if everything has returned to the correct location. Or worse, it could be hard for you to tell if your doctor returned your bits and pieces back to the right spots.

Before you jump to any depressing conclusions, you might want to wait a few weeks or even months before taking a gander, when things aren't as swollen or sore, and your vagina looks a bit more familiar and not like something that's been to war and back. Also, if you haven't trimmed the hedges in a few months, trying to locate your own sexual stimulation buttons might be moot. You're women, not jungle explorers, ladies, and you certainly don't have time to engage in some sort of nether region expedition. Nor do you want to get distracted by your mini-rain forest. And if things are completely overgrown, you won't be able to accurately assess their current status.

So if you're looking to take a welcome-back tour of your own private parts, you'll probably want to ensure that you can actually find them yourself. Because if you can't find them, don't expect your partner—you know, the guy whose underwear can't seem to find the large white laundry basket in the corner of your bedroom—to be able to easily locate them either. And considering men tend to never stop for directions, you could be in for a very long night. It's best to give them explicit guidance and an easy-to-read map before they dive in.

RE-ENERGIZING YOUR BUNNY

Once you can find your vagina, attempting to get her back up to speed is a whole other ballgame. Postpartum hormones, particularly the ones that support breastfeeding and milk production, can chap even the most luscious of vaginal lips, leaving many women totally dry even after a long marathon of foreplay sessions. You'll need more than a tube of ChapStick to remedy this lovely side effect.

And then after you've bought stock in four different brands of lube, your vagina starts leaking more than your boobs. Apparently, you should have registered for panty liners. They're every mom's new must-have accessory.

And if that's not enough, your usually taut vagina is now randomly dropping tampons, and you realize that either everything is "pee-your-pants" funny, or you've just joined the ranks of thousands of incontinent senior citizens and postpartum mothers in this country. Except unlike your grandmother, you're in your mid-thirties and they don't make thong-shaped Depends just yet.

The good news is that you're not alone; many women report at least one if not many changes to their nether regions after having a baby, most of which can be easily remedied. So pick yourself up by your sagging labia and get ready to start fresh.

GOOD GIRLS HAVE PUBES

If you've been carrying a baby around for nine months, you're probably in need of some expert hedge trimming. Think about it. If a new 'do down below can work the same magic as a fabulous new haircut up above, then it might be worth the effort.

Now, if your pubic hair has gotten out of hand, don't be embarrassed. Unless you're on hiatus from Cirque du Soleil, there's just no way to take good care of it on your own. But now you don't really have an excuse. Well, you sort of do, but at least you can put the baby down now, so Junior is no longer completely blocking your view.

If you're not concerned about what's going on down below or just haven't had time to look, here are some possible signs that it might be time to pay a little more attention to your pubic hairstyling:

- You look like you have more than a vagina in your pants.
- You have oddly gone up an underwear size.
- You could easily sport cornrows . . . down below.

- You could catch small woodland animals in your bush.
- Your trimmings constitute an adequate Locks of Love donation.
- Your partner needs a comb to part the "waters" in order to provide you with oral pleasure.
- You find an astonishing number of hairballs throughout your house. And you don't own a cat.

If any or all of these scenarios apply to you, then you should really consider doing some crotch-hair coiffing.

Now before you get your curlies in a tightly knotted wad, keep in mind that this doesn't mean that you've got to take the Britney Spears approach to their Ronald McDonald. In fact, many women feel strongly about their right to go untamed and au naturel. Apparently some women don't necessarily want to look like porn stars, at least when it comes to their crotches. And sure, like anything else, your crotch couture is your personal preference. But if you've always sported a full bush, you just never know what a shave could do for your overall sexual experience.

When asked about going bald down below, many women talk about how much their husbands would love for them to do it. And sure, since pubic hair rarely makes more than a cameo in a porno or sex magazine, you could see why dudes might think it's sexy.

But c'mon, moms. While it's a nice gesture to surprise your partner with a new look, that shouldn't be your sole motivation. Who says a shorter 'do is solely for the pleasure and enjoyment of your significant other? Perhaps your partner enjoys picking hair from his teeth or likes the tickle of pubes in his throat. And nothing says "sexy mama" like stray hairs creeping down your thighs and poking through your panties.

The truth is that when you decide to make a change to your pubic hair, it's not just about putting out a "Welcome Oral Sex" mat for your partner. It can make you feel sexier, fresher, and in some cases, a few pounds lighter. And generally speaking, it takes way less time keeping up a cleanly shaven look than it does trying to trim, cut, and style a natural bush. Most moms have a hard time trying to use the bathroom alone, so adding in a good hour of lady-scaping is probably not an option. With your new schedule, you're lucky to shave your pits and put on deodorant, let alone take time every week to trim, clip, and manicure your pubic hair.

MOMINATRIX **SAYS**

Not convinced yet? Know that many women report that without all the excess hair down below, they can better experience all that pleasurable friction that occurs during sex.

Now entering into the world of crotch-hair couture is not something to be taken lightly. Maybe you've heard horror stories of razor burn and nicks in the most inconvenient of places, or you've had visions of a scary woman in white pouring wax over your blessed crotch and ripping our hair out while laughing heartily as you cringe in pain. But before you completely wimp out and cry "uncle," remember that you birthed a baby—and maybe even dealt with a sick and teething one for longer than twenty-four straight hours—which really means that having hair ripped out of your anus is more like a day at the spa for you. Plus you'll need completely uninterrupted no-kid time to get the job done. And most moms would agree that breaks like those are practically orgasmic.

Shaving

While an ominous task at first, shaving is a viable option for moms who just don't have the opportunity to have someone else take care of things for them, which is code for being afraid of the scary woman in white and her big pot of wax. Don't fool yourself. The initial shave could take longer than the labor of your first child, so be prepared. Get a babysitter, rent a Shop-Vac, and take your time. If your hair is longer than a quarter inch, you will want to trim with scissors or clippers before trying to shave. There's just no razor that can take on dreadlocks or a 'fro, so take charge of it before you shave it.

MOMINATRIX SAYS

Invest in clear shaving gel and a good mirror, or grab a Schick Intuition razor with the lotion already built right in. It makes things a lot easier, and will hopefully eliminate the chance of an embarrassing ER visit.

Once you've got the initial shave under your belt, the upkeep isn't as difficult as you might imagine. Most moms who shave just do it every single time they're in the shower. Start with your legs and simply keep going up—with the grain of the hair, of course. Let the warm water run for a bit to open your follicles and soften the hair. And make sure you've got a good shaving gel, a top-notch single-bladed razor, a handy mirror, a set of scissors, and some clippers around. Depending on your skill level, you might want to enlist the help of your partner (who might find this incredibly titillating).

Although the act of shaving can be sexually stimulating, total smoothness (if you can even achieve that) only lasts for a good six hours. The biggest challenge by far is your undercarriage and inner lips, both of which are not the easiest to see, let alone shave with a sharp object. Even with lots of practice and experience, it's nearly impossible to quickly and easily shave those tricky parts. So if you're determined to get a completely shaved bush every single time, then you're going to have to be willing to spend some extra time. And even then, you're probably going to end up with a stray hair or ten. It's just the nature of the beast.

So, if you're not a frequent shower-taker or shaver, this is probably not the right method for you. However, if you can get a smooth shave on your legs, and you can make crotch couture a fixture in your regular routine, it's definitely the cheapest and quickest option.

Waxing

There are lots of products out there, including the actual wax that spas and salons use, that will allow you to wax yourself. And sure, it might be a cheaper and more convenient option, but your vagina is not something to experiment on. Your mono-brow is one thing, but your pubic hair might be something to leave to the professionals.

It's imperative that you find a legitimate establishment—or better, a personal recommendation from a friend. You probably wouldn't trust just anyone to cut or color your hair, so it doesn't make sense to choose some random person at a strip mall to rip out your pubes. If none of your friends have yet to make the leap to Brazil, then use the trusty Internet to find reviews.

Before your appointment, make sure you've got at least a quarter-inch of hair. Still, it shouldn't be *too* long; if you can braid your bush, you should trim before you go. Depending on your comfort level, your esthetician will actually do the pre-wax haircut for you, which will save you time and the annoying bathroom floor cleanup.

If you tend to be sensitive to people ripping your hair out of your crotch, then taking a mild pain reliever prior to the visit will help, especially if you are pregnant or immediately postpartum.

Now, when you schedule your appointment, make sure you specify what you want. At the same time, remember that you can always request more or less during the visit, depending on how things go. Here are a few definitions for you:

- *Bikini Wax:* This is just the hair outside the line where your bikini would show. The bikini line can vary greatly depending on the estheticians, so be sure to ask where they draw the line (literally). If it's too much or not enough, just let them know.
- *Half Brazilian:* This is all the hair on the outer lips.

- *Full Brazilian or "Porn Star Special":* If you're happy having those few stray hairs on your asshole, then make sure you let her know. And you might want to do a few stretches before your appointment, since you'll have to flip your legs around in all sorts of positions for the esthetician to get you nice and clean.

MOMINATRIX **SAYS**

Strips or Wax on Wax?—that is the question. While the paper strips are quicker and cover a lot more surface area, many women swear that the wax on wax hurts less. They do require more rips, since they don't cover as much surface area, but they can be more accurate, which does reduce ingrown hairs.

When you arrive for your appointment, you have three options. You can decide to leave on your own underwear, wear the lovely paper panties they provide, or just go naked. If you're getting more than an edge cleanup, you're going to have to let everything out anyway, so keep that in mind when you decide to tightly cling to your underpants. Estheticians are completely professional, and you'll be surprised as to how unsexual the entire experience is. The ripping of the hair usually takes away any sense of eroticism you might have been worried about.

The level of pain varies, and many women report that it's actually less painful than a facial waxing. You are getting your crotch hair ripped out, however, so don't expect a tickle or pluck. But it can be worth being without kids or any distractions for a full forty-five minutes, even if you are completely naked in a brightly lit room with some random person staring at your vagina.

Some women feel a bit too naked with all their hair gone, so they ask for a bit of hair to be left intact. This is otherwise known as a "landing strip." Depending on how modest you are, you can instruct your friendly esthetician as to how much or how little you'd like.

Expect tenderness and redness for a couple of hours after your appointment is over. Most experienced professionals will treat your newly hairless pubic area with lotions that will help speed the recovery process.

Keep in mind that you won't have to return for at least another four weeks to have the procedure done again, in which time all the sex you'll be having will make it extremely worth it.

MOMINATRIX SAYS

Pubic hair does happen to prevent friction between your vagina and your panties, so if you choose to lose the bush, make sure you wear breathable fabrics like cotton and silk.

Hair Removal Lotions

Any stinky chemical that melts away hair and includes a warning label the size of a shopping list, along with a time limit before "skin will become red and raw," should be enough to make you grab a razor. Add your crotch into the mix and it's probably safer for you, your skin, and the ozone to pull out your hair with tweezers. In a few words: Just say no!

If you're feeling brave, you'll want to make sure you test the product out on another part of your body before you head south with it. And you'll want to be extra careful that the product does not go anywhere inside your vagina. Most of these products, if not all, are made for outer use only. And for a good reason.

The Nitty Gritty on Regrowth

For some reason, whenever you mention shaving or waxing, people freak out about ingrown hairs and regrowth. Both are legitimate concerns, but nothing that should keep you from giving the clean shave or wax a try.

You'll find a plethora of after-wax and after-shave treatments for women that can do wonders in easing any pain, discomfort, swelling, or itching you might have. Most of these lotions contain Aloe Vera. If you are prone to ingrown hairs, mention that to your esthetician, who may use a wax on wax method instead of strips. While it might take a bit longer, it usually provides a cleaner and more thorough wax.

Make sure you exfoliate often, particularly before you shave or wax, but in between sessions as well. You'll also want to give your hair a chance to grow in a bit before shaving or waxing again. This ensures that the hair is just long enough and strong enough to be properly cut or pulled out.

And contrary to old wives' tales and your own mother, shaved or waxed hair does not grow back quicker or thicker. Actually, more frequent and regularly scheduled waxing can actually make your hair follicles thinner and less noticeable.

THE MOMINATRIX'S CROTCH COUTURE CHEAT SHEET		
Shaving	**Pros:** Cheap, convenient, generally painless, can do easily at home	**Cons:** Lots of upkeep, doesn't last long, difficult getting the undercarriage, regrowth can be itchy
Hair Removal Lotions	**Pros:** Melting your hair off with chemicals can be fun to watch if you're into that sort of thing	**Cons:** Chemicals, chemicals, burning, stinging, chemicals
Waxing	**Pros:** Gets you out of house, neat and clean, lasts for a long time, even appearance	**Cons:** Can be painful, requires an appointment and therefore childcare, and can result in ingrown hairs

THE DOUBLE Ds: DRYNESS AND DISCHARGE

Now that you're sporting a brand new hairdo or bald bush and looking spiffy on the outside, you've got to tackle your vagina's inner beauty, or what could be called "The Double Ds": dryness and discharge.

Dry as a Bone

As many new moms are forewarned, the postpartum hormone progesterone that's responsible for supporting the production of breastmilk, coupled with a deficit in the estrogen department, will almost instantly dry you out.

You probably remember your midwife or doctor warning you with the "make sure you buy some lube" speech, but considering you were still worrying about having to poop, let alone have sex, you probably ignored them and went back to figuring out how propping your feet up on a stool is supposed to help what feels like a second childbirth on the toilet.

The truth is that vaginal dryness is a huge complaint among postpartum women, but it is often the most misunderstood, particularly by sex-hungry partners who have been ever so patiently waiting for that six-week "open for business" mark. If you haven't figured it out already, no amount of foreplay or oral sex will provide you with the adequate lubrication that you will need to make early postpartum sex remotely comfortable.

While it is possible to produce lubrication, particularly for women who are not breastfeeding, that doesn't mean you'll create enough to last you longer than the first few moments after entry. And while you can mask your yelps of pain as cries of pleasure, it's not worth it in the long run; not only will you be walking even more like you just rode a horse for three weeks, but you'll be less likely to want to try it again in the next century.

MOMINATRIX SAYS

Do not pretend to enjoy something if it really does hurt. Vaginal dryness can be fairly easily remedied, so there's just no reason to grin and bear it.

Postpartum vaginal dryness can be particularly hard for male partners with big egos who are convinced that just a little more of "this" and a lot more of "that" will turn your faucet on. But this reaction will get you both nowhere. Just save yourselves some trouble, invest in some lube, and be free with it. No need to worry about some sort of lube drought in the lower forty-nine states anytime soon. There's plenty of lube to go around. And make sure you put down some towels before you get hot and heavy. You're probably already swimming in a bed full of new and exciting fluids. There's no reason to add one more to the mix.

If you don't address your dryness, it can definitely be a source of vaginal pain during sex. Of course, postpartum vaginal pain can also be your body's way of telling you that you're just not ready for sex yet, or it can be a symptom of a bigger problem involving everything from a bruised cervix to incorrectly placed stitches. So if you've passed the six-week window, are using lots of lube, and are still experiencing discomfort, talk to your doctor or midwife. You just had a baby; you most certainly do not need any more pain down there, especially when it comes to something that's supposed to provide you with a ridiculous amount of pleasure.

The Drip

Once you've dealt with your bout of vaginal dryness and invested stock in lube, you'll soon discover your overabundance of vaginal discharge, also known as *leucorrhea*. Just think of all the cute and funny songs your kids could come up with that.

It's one of the many ironies of a mother's existence. If you can get past the name, then you'll realize that leucorrhea is caused by all those extra hormones, which are trying to do something other than making you cry at random greeting cards and paper towel commercials. But instead of regenerating into brain cells or shrinking your stomach into a perfect vision of six-pack abs, it creates an overabundance of vaginal discharge or "natural lubricant."

Perhaps you've been out at the store or at the playground with your baby. Suddenly, you feel like you're starting your period. Then you discover a large gob of creamy white or yellow goo staring up at you from your underpants. That's leucorrhea.

Of course, it comes at the most inopportune of times—*not* when you'd most appreciate having a little extra moisture. As a result, many women feel more comfortable sporting their favorite panty liner to prevent that not-so-dry feeling throughout the day.

MOMINATRIX SAYS

While excess discharge is sadly par for the course, if it's got a strong odor and causes you vaginal discomfort, make sure to have it checked out by your doctor or midwife.

Unfortunately, there's little you can do to remedy the situation, other than complain about it to your friends and stock up on panty liners. Another solution, of course, is to change your underpants on what can be an hourly basis. But considering you're already busy changing your kid's diaper every hour, that may not seem like the best option. Plus, there's no need to add more to your already ridiculously large laundry pile.

WHY BIGGER ISN'T ALWAYS BETTER

So your crotch is reacting to childbirth like a proverbial vaginal *el niño*. And if that's not annoying enough, you just figured out that your doctor doesn't need a speculum for your six-week exam, and you don't need the string to get your tampons out anymore. And you thought stretch marks were bad.

Quite frankly, women who have not had a vaginal birth will probably not experience as much of a change as those who have shot a baby or two out of their vag. Consider yourselves lucky, you c-section bitches. It doesn't take a rocket scientist to figure out that if you've birthed a few seven- or eight-pounders, your vagina will not return to its trim and virginal state without some effort. And even then, it might still be somewhat of a lost cause.

The Vaginal Exercise of Champions

Sadly, it does make sense that if your vaginal muscles get stretched and used, and you don't do anything to get it back in shape—you know, like Kegels—it's probably not going to return to its normal state. You shouldn't need a college degree to figure out that one.

Of course, no doctor ever tells you that doing Kegels will allow you to maintain some sense of postpartum dignity. Kegels tend to take a back burner to all the other four thousand things moms-to-be are thinking about prior to having a baby. And then after the baby arrives, moms are much less apt to remember to do their Kegels because they're losing brain matter through their breastmilk or getting burned out thanks to lack of adequate sleep. But then they start peeing themselves when absolutely no laughter is involved, and they figure out that even the extra-super-duper tampons don't seem to fit anymore. Unfortunately, there's only so much that pre- and postpartum Kegels can do. Your vagina may never be exactly the same as it was before you pushed a large baby through it. That's not to say Kegels won't help you. But know that many women do find that their vagina becomes increasingly less taut after each child.

MOMINATRIX SAYS

So maybe incontinence isn't enough motivation to get you to do your Kegels. But did you know that these muscles are responsible for orgasms, ladies? The stronger the muscles, the better the climax.

Now almost every single pregnancy and new-mom book will divulge some series of Kegel exercises. These range from a strict Baby Boot Camp–type of regimen to the more casual approach that involves doing them every time you think about how painful your labor will be. You don't need Tae-Bo Kegel or Kegeling to the oldies; just remember to do them. If you're still pregnant, tie a string around your swollen finger or make a daily date with Kegel in your appointment book. Or better yet, make a game out of it and Kegel every time someone says a specific word during your favorite television show. Hell, you can't play drinking games anymore, so turn them into Kegel games. Your continence should be enough to move Kegels a bit higher on your "baby preparation list." Baby bedding lasts a good year, tops. Your vagina is with you forever.

Just because you've got a baby in your arms and not in your belly doesn't mean you still can't and shouldn't Kegel. The vagina is a muscle, after all, so if you don't give her a little workout, she's not going to hold onto her girlish "figure" forever.

Meet Your New Friend, Ben-Wa

Lest you and your forlorn vagina be discouraged, many women report excellent results from Ben-Wa balls, a sex-toy-slash-vaginal-exercise-apparatus that can provide you with equal parts tautness and pleasure. There are varying types, shapes, and sizes of Ben-Wa balls. However, the Smart Balls are generally the best because they are ergonomically shaped and easy to clean. Simply insert one at a time, squeeze your PC muscle, you know, the one that you use when you need to stop yourself from peeing, and then pull gently on the string. Rumor has it that these exercises can be much more exciting with balls that vibrate.

MOMINATRIX SAYS

Try using a little lube and only one Ben-Wa ball for your first go. Once you feel comfortable and stronger, up the ante.

If you're staring at the balls thinking that they couldn't possibly both fit up there, then just take a glance over at that cute little thing babbling next to you. If Junior came out, then those Ben-Wa balls can most certainly go in.

Going Under the Knife

And finally, if desperation has totally set in and your childbearing days are officially over, you could always invest in a vaginal rejuvenation procedure. For a fairly hefty price, you can have some friendly doctor laser your vaginal walls and tighten your girl up. While this may sound a bit extreme, the prospect of walking around with a gaping hole in your undercarriage might just be the motivation you need.

Plastic surgery of any kind should not be taken lightly. As with any surgical procedure, risks of various kinds are involved and should be researched thoroughly. It's always best to interview doctors and talk to patients who have had this procedure done.

And keep in mind that while it's true that vaginas get more than their fair share of a workout during labor and delivery, parenting and sleep deprivation can certainly do a number on a dick. So while you might be stretched out, chances are, he's probably got some shrinkage.

5

BRINGING YOUR SEXY BACK

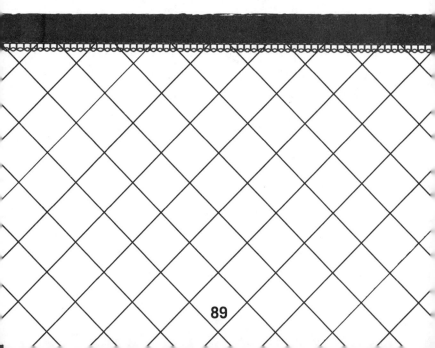

As if labor and delivery weren't traumatic enough, one long look at yourself in the mirror might just be enough to send you right back into the hospital. Whether you've got an easy baby or one that's more like a rabid bear cub, you are now someone's bitch—one part wet nurse, one part handmaiden— with no fairy godmother to be found. So the only time you get to take care of yourself is after you've completed all your chores. And when you have the choice between catching a few winks or taking a shower and getting gussied up, you'll probably pick a few hours of sleep on any day.

Consequently, everything from your brows to your beaver has probably grown like weeds, and the circles under your eyes and stubborn baby weight have made you almost unrecognizable, even to yourself. Add that all together and you've got the perfect recipe for celibacy.

You shouldn't be surprised that the road to your sexual desire and satisfaction is paved in a healthy self-esteem and body image, both of which are probably a bit shell-shocked thanks to pregnancy and childbirth. The yo-yo of weight gain and loss, combined with your inability to spend the attention you need on looking and feeling great, are enough to knock the wind right out of your already fragile self-image.

Unfortunately, moms generally spend most of their time and energy on their kids, and they rarely do enough for themselves. But when it comes down to it, if you're not taking care of yourself, you're not helping your kid. Happy moms make for much happier babies and kids. And while you might think that spending every single waking moment with your child is your motherly duty, the baby is probably just as tired of looking at your mug as you are of staring at Junior's screaming mouth. This is not permission to drop everything and head to a Mexican spa resort for some immediate pampering, but perhaps it might be time to quit treating yourself like an afterthought and spend a little more than a few spare guilt-ridden minutes tending to yourself.

If you haven't figured it out yet, the dutiful act of mothering—and all the ass wiping and drool catching that comes along with it—is not inherently sexy. Shocking as it may sound, you just don't see men pining after the bedraggled postpartum mother who hasn't showered in four days.

Part of merging the woman you were and the mom you are now is letting your sexual being rise up from behind the stretch marks and the hemorrhoids and take back a bit of what's rightfully yours.

THE FIRST SIX WEEKS

When it comes to those early postpartum weeks, definitely try to maintain an "anything goes" type of attitude. Think of yourself as a soldier in the trenches of motherhood; the most basic human functions become small luxuries. So focus on feeling better, both mentally and physically; getting as much sleep as you possibly can; and keeping your baby's butt dry and mouth fed. Celebrate diaper changes that didn't end up in massive explosions and mid-day baths. Be glad for days when you are able to survive with only one good cry. At this stage, showers and general self-care are almost optional, and really, if you're able to feed, clothe, and potty yourself (and your baby), you're doing a fantastic job.

There are a few things that you can do to help decrease the likelihood of a crying spell (your own, that is). For one thing, don't look in the mirror. You do not need to let the reality of your current state have any time to actually soak in. Invest in some hair elastics or a few hats and call it a day. Put your makeup away and just opt for a good face wash and antiwrinkle cream.

If you cry more than once or let your kid sit in poop for longer than Junior would probably prefer, don't beat yourself up about it. Tomorrow is a completely new day that you haven't had a chance to screw up just yet.

THE MOMMY UNIFORM

While the "mommy uniform" has certainly evolved over the years from the matching tracksuit to the yoga pants and T-shirt combination, it's still never flattering. (Well, unless you're a yoga instructor.) Sorry, moms. But not all women's asses are created equal.

So while it might appear that grabbing a T-shirt and sweatpants (whatever your version of those might be) and slapping them on your body to leave the house is the easiest way to go, it's really just as easy to grab something that's both stylish and simple. Plus, you'll stop looking like a gym rat.

Under no circumstances should you attempt to try on any pre-pregnancy clothes. Just relegate yourself to your maternity wear until you're past the first six weeks. The last thing you want to do is grab your favorite pair of jeans in a size you haven't worn in almost a year and try to squeeze your ass into them. No good can come from that.

If your maternity pants are sliding off your butt, you might actually be ready to try on regular clothes, but use extreme caution when attempting to reacclimatize your body back to the world of non-maternity clothing. It's actually best to hit a store and try on clothes a few sizes up from your typical size. Aim high so that you can ease yourself into the depression that comes with not fitting into clothes anywhere near your regular size. It's always better for something to be too big than for you to have to ask the dressing room attendant for help getting out of your clothes.

MOMINATRIX SAYS

Make a promise to yourself that you will not purchase any maternity clothing after you've had the baby. No matter how desperate you are, there's just no reason to move backward when it comes to your wardrobe.

The first few months are incredibly frustrating in the clothes department, mainly because once you're ready to get yourself out of the stretch pants and oversized shirts, you can't find anything that fits. You might be a Gap girl up top and a Lane Bryant lady on the bottom, neither of which make for a quick and easy shopping trip. If only you had four hours and a personal assistant to help you try on clothes. If you do find clothes that fit you, there's still a great chance that you'll be swimming in them in just a couple of months, so remember that now you may be spending money on something you're only going to wear for a short chunk of time.

You probably don't want to buy a hundred-dollar pair of jeans, but it is worth dropping a few bucks on one or two go-to outfits that you can wear if you do get the opportunity to leave the house. If you're headed back to work, you can always visit a local consignment shop; you might not feel as bad spending money on used clothes that you're going to shrink out of soon (fingers crossed).

MOMINATRIX SAYS

A good rule of thumb is that if you wear it to bed, then you can't wear it outside.

Also, wearing items that are still a few sizes up from your typical one doesn't mean you haven't lost any weight. You did have a seven- or eight-pound baby, right? But keep in mind that your hips are completely out of whack and your belly was stretched out a good half foot, so you're going to need the extra room.

MuuMuus Are so 1972

Just because you're spending your days and nights housebound does not mean you need to look like it. When you're stuck in the house for most of the day, it's really easy to fall into a comfortable clothing rut, which many moms interpret as free rein to sport gaucho pants and old T-shirts everyday. Regardless of whether you're Angelina Jolie or not, it's pretty damn hard to feel hot in an old ratty T-shirt and sweatpants, let alone have someone else think you're sexy.

Sure, the daddy tees and gym shorts are great for the first few days. Plus, they will allow you to spend all your money on the expensive baby bedding and forty-dollar Onesies that your baby will outgrow in the next fourteen minutes. But if a pair of yoga pants and slightly fitted T-shirt is considered "dressed up" for you, or your partner doesn't recognize you when you put on a pair of jeans and a real shirt, then you might want to consider a few better options.

Thankfully, nursing gowns and pjs have made great strides over the last few years, and you should most certainly take advantage of these design changes. Do not be swayed by the shapeless nightgowns with gaping holes for your milk-laden breasts, or the goofy flannel pajamas smothered in flying sheep. You can still be comfortable without looking like you stepped right out of a Sears catalog.

Rest assured that you'll feel just as great in your stylish attire. And the best part is that if you pick carefully and accessorize accordingly, you might be able to leave the house in them without being picked up by the *What Not to Wear* team.

THE MOMINATRIX'S TOP THREE PICKS FOR AROUND-THE-HOUSE NURSING GOWNS		
Boob	www.boobdesign.com	Leave it to the Europeans to state the obvious. Simple design that's easy to use and easy on the eyes.
Majamas	www.majamas.com	These super-comfortable mom pajamas and nursing gowns are nice enough to wear out of the house. Well, at least to check the mail.
Japanese Weekend	www.japaneseweekend.com	Known for their smart maternity wear, they make nursing gear that is just as intelligent and comfortable without the frump.

The Babydoll Dress and Leggings

Now, before you go running for the hills, proclaiming your disdain and disgust for leggings, keep in mind that when paired with a dress and some comfortable flats, rather than a short boxy top and a pair of neon heels, it's completely different than anything you might have sported in the 1980s. The look itself is extremely mom-friendly, and styles such as trapeze, empire waist, or wrap (if you're breastfeeding) are easy to find at any clothing store. Not only do the leggings help keep everything contained, but the dress itself does wonders in covering everything discretely and stylishly. You'll be comfortable enough to roll around on the floor with your toddler but still dressed up enough to avoid looking like you just left the gym.

Mominatrix SAYS

To dress up this look for evenings, grab a pair of Spanx footless tights (*www.spanx.com*). Add some sexy heels, and kill two birds (or two rolls) with one stone.

The key to pulling off the look is to make sure the dress is actually something you might wear without the leggings, which means knee length or just barely above the knee. If you wouldn't be caught dead in it without anything underneath, then it's too short. Also, you'll want to grab styles that don't make you look pregnant. There's a fine line between a cute, stylish babydoll dress and a maternity one. If you're not completely sure, bring a few home and try them on for a friend or your partner. You can't rely on the eighteen-year-old salesgirl to tell you that you look like you're due in a few months.

Dresses used to be completely off limits for nursing moms, but thanks to a simple crossover and low-v neckline, you'll be able to find a plethora of dresses that will allow you to nurse without having to strip down naked. And if the babydoll style doesn't appeal to you or isn't as flattering as it should be, play around with different dress styles. While button-down fronts can work, they can take a while to open, especially if you're trying to unbutton them with one hand. Wrap dresses flatter any shape or size, and they also allow for easy breastfeeding access.

Accessories, Accessories

If you're feeling bitter about your limited wardrobe, then spice it up with a few accessories. Not only are they one-size-fits-all, which makes them a great long-term investment, but they can help you take your boring outfit and add a stylish flair without spending hundreds of dollars on a new wardrobe.

Mominatrix SAYS

In general, nursing necklaces and teething jewelry suck. Just give your kid a teether or rattle and keep your jewelry for yourself.

Jewelry

Trade in your teeny gold chain or diamond studs for a bit of costume jewelry. Before you get Liberace in your head, realize that costume jewelry is just code for "not that expensive." Department stores such as Target are stocked full of trendy bracelets, necklaces, earrings, and rings, all of which will spice up your boring T-shirt and jeans, and let you express yourself without breaking your bank.

Generally speaking, go for pairings (not sets), such as earrings and a bracelet, or a necklace and a ring, instead of a bunch of pieces piled on all at once. Do not feel obligated to match perfectly. Your grandmother's jewelry rules are long gone. And don't be afraid of big. It might actually take away the focus from your belly or ass. And carefully chosen pieces, save the dangling earrings (watch out!), can help occupy your kids in desperate times.

Diaper Bags

Your pre-baby bag obsession does not have to be curtailed once you have a kid. Actually, you may find that your penchant for designer bags is easily translated to diaper bags, many of which are so fantastic that you wouldn't even know they were diaper bags, except for the diapers inside them. Imagine that. Whether you love rich patent leather or are drawn to bright cheery fabrics, you will find a bag (or twelve) in various sizes, shapes, and styles that you'd actually carry even if you had not just popped out a baby. Except, unlike a regular old purse, most come complete with a changing pad and four hundred pouches for pacifiers, teethers, and snack containers. Plus, they are easy to clean and maintain.

THE MOMINATRIX'S TOP FIVE DIAPER BAGS THAT DON'T LOOK LIKE DIAPER BAGS

Nest	www.nestchildren.com	These big, stylish bags have been seen on the shoulders of Heidi Klum and for good reason. They've got tons of room for all things baby, but the gorgeous leather construction makes them look like any hot and trendy designer bag.
Pinnington	www.pinningtonbags.com	These look a bit more like traditional diaper bags, but they appeal to the Bohemian set with amazing plush fabrics and deep outer topics. You'll swoon over the brightly colored and completely waterproof inner lining.
Orla Kiely	www.orlakiely.com	While Orla's bags aren't technically diaper bags, they're fully lined and extremely durable, both important qualities of a mom-friendly bag. And if you're completely averse to the idea of carrying a diaper bag, then you won't feel like you're compromising with this slung over your arm.
Baby Kaed	www.babykaed.com	With a wide selection of bags for every taste, these mom-designed bags come complete with everything you'd generally have to find yourself and stuff into your bag, such as a changing pad, cell phone holder, wet bag, and wipes case.
The Chaiken Diaper Bag	www.saksfifthavenue.com	If you've got a bunch of hundreds just lying around waiting to be spent, then The Chaiken Diaper Bag should be at the top of your list.

Undergarments

Even if you're still wearing maternity clothes well after the first six weeks have passed, you can definitely invest in better undergarments. For the most part, postpartum underwear isn't even fit for dust cloths. Once you've gotten your use out of the "pad holders," just toss them. It's amazing what a new pair of panties can do for your self-esteem and your ass. That certainly does not mean you'll be sporting your low-rider thongs anytime soon, but clearly anything is probably better than what you've been trying to pass off as underwear.

C-section moms might have a more difficult time with the underwear issue, mainly because even after you get your staples out, your incision will probably still be a little weepy, making bathroom trips a bit more uncomfortable than you'd ever prefer. In your case, you might consider a couple of special panties, including a C-Panty (*www.cpanty.com*), which features a silicone lining so your incision won't stick, and Czela Bellies (*www.czelablue.com*), which have a fuzzy strip inside the waistband to provide comfort when your incision has fully healed but is still a bit sensitive. Both brands provide you with some much needed comfort without screaming "special mommy underpants."

Bras can be a bit more complicated, particularly if you're breastfeeding. Not only can it be difficult to figure out your size, but it's pretty hard to feel sexy when, at the least, you've got a cotton pad stuffed over your nipples, and in many cases, some type of cold or hot pad to soothe them.

You should not feel as though you're stuck with gigantic ugly nursing bras that should never ever see the light of day lest they scare small children and sweet old women. Thankfully, there have been huge advances in the nursing bra world. Not only are they almost pretty in style and construction, but they can even be downright sexy. And while you'll want a bra that does provide you with easy nipple access, keep a few non-nursing bras around. When you're on the town without your baby, you won't need a nursing bra, but chances are high that your old ones (if you can find them) won't fit you anyway. Just pretend that you've got a whole new set of ta-tas, and use them as an excuse to get some brand-new bras.

Body Slimmers

Why is it that moms will hit the grocery store in an old pair of sweats and a baseball cap, and yet they feel ashamed to grab any type of undergarment slimming product? Look, ladies. If they're good enough for Oprah and every other celebrity out there (yes, even the skinny ones), then they should most certainly be good enough for you. Not only can they make the difference between keeping you in maternity jeans and allowing you to slip into a pair of regular-sized pants, but they just make everything, even those crappy T-shirts, fit better. And rumor has it that they can even drop you down a size or two. Sold!

The fairly lumpy and bumpy postpartum body can be extremely disconcerting, even if you're wearing loose clothing, so invest in some Spanx (*www.spanx.com*). You'll get a tummy tuck without the sharp knife, heavy drugs, and hefty price tag. And you'll rid yourself of the dreaded muffin top. Besides, with everything tucked comfortably in your body slimmer, you might be more inclined to experiment with your current wardrobe. And then you can finally stop worrying that some idiot is going to ask you when you're expecting again.

MOMINATRIX SAYS

Spanx can be a little pricey, so make sure to check out their more economical line, "Assets," at your local Target.

THE TRIFECTA OF GETTING LAID: HAIR—FACE—BODY

The right clothes and undergarments won't do anything for your overall sex appeal if you're wearing your hair in a big greasy rat's nest on top of your head and your feet are so rough you could draw blood from your partner with one accidental scrape. Just because you had a baby does not mean you shouldn't be able to maintain the basic human requirements of showering, shaving, and fixing some type of hairstyle other than a ponytail. Once you feel comfortable leaving the baby, for God's sake, go get your hair done.

The Mommy 'Do

Before you run off and get the desperate "mommy, do," which is generally some type of awful hack job, take a few minutes to chat with your hairstylist about what works for your face and your lifestyle. Make sure to be clear about the amount of time you're willing to spend on your hair before you let the stylist do anything to it. The last thing you need is something that requires a full blow dry and flat iron. There are plenty of hairstyles out there that won't take you long to do, but that also won't age you a good twenty years. And if you've got an extra few minutes, get a quick eyebrow and lip wax (if that applies to you).

Putting on Your Face

Now when it comes to makeup, it's a complete and total myth that you need more than five minutes to put on a decent face. Clearly you may have to get rid of a couple of steps in your typical makeup regimen, but you won't sacrifice anything but a few layers of goop that you probably didn't even need anyway.

MOMINATRIX SAYS

It may sound scary, but you might want to invest in a dry shampoo like Klorane. It's a mom's best friend.

Just to add insult to injury, motherhood often brings skin problems and other facial issues that you may not have had before. The puffy tired eyes, weird pregnancy acne, and plain old (and often strategically placed) wrinkles might be tough to handle in the few minutes that you have available to you. However, that doesn't mean you should just ignore them and hope that people will be mesmerized by your baby and not notice the fact that you look like someone punched you in both eyes before you left the house. Babies, particularly cute and nicely dressed ones, can definitely work as a distraction tactic, but inevitably, someone will take a gander at you.

If your face hasn't seen makeup since you could see your feet, you might want to toss it out and start fresh. Besides the fact that makeup shopping is a fantastic baby diversion—and you can certainly use all the fun you can get—you're only going to need a few items, some of which actually expire. Don't be swayed by makeup that is specifically marketed to moms. Unless those kits include more hours in the day and an actual makeup artist, just pass and go with a brand that's healthy for your skin, good for your face, and doesn't make you look like you just had a Mary Kay consultation. And you've already got enough shit that screams "mommy," so you don't need your face powder to say it along with everything else in your bag.

MOMINATRIX SAYS

Many times, pregnancy-induced skin issues will resolve themselves during the early postpartum months. But if not, make an appointment with a dermatologist. The last thing you need to deal with during the newborn months (and beyond) is crappy skin.

The Mominatrix's Five-Minute Mom Face

1. Apply a face lotion with SPF (tinted if you need to even out your skin tone). Applying lotion just ensures that your makeup won't be gone after the first hour. You can certainly use a foundation or base if you need extra coverage, but if you're going for fast, then you don't have time to worry about blending.

2. Use a cream blush. Pick a color that's a bit brighter than you might normally choose, and rub it on the apple of your cheeks. You want the look of a flushed, love-struck teen—not a little girl who got into her mother's makeup bag.

3. In order to keep everything from running down your face or disappearing in a matter of a few hours, dust your face with a translucent power. It will also take care of the shine that many oily faced moms still suffer from.

4. Grab a black mascara and coat your upper lashes, preferably ones that have been curled. Do your lower lashes for a more sophisticated look or if you have an extra twenty seconds.

5. Applying a regular lipstick might make you look like a streetwalker, so take the subtle route with a lightly shaded gloss or lip balm. You can reapply it as often as necessary, and best of all, you won't need a mirror.

Ways to Lose the Weight

Regardless of whether you worked out until the day you went into labor, or you haven't seen the inside of a gym since you were in elementary school, dropping the pregnancy pounds can present a bit of a challenge when you're at the whim of a needy baby whose main goal in life seems to be to suck the energy right out of you. But a diet plan that consists of grabbing whatever you can rip open and microwave before the baby wakes up, and a work-out regimen that involves carrying, bouncing, or nursing Junior all night long might not be enough to get you out of the trapeze shirts and elastic-waist pants.

Thankfully, once you adapt to the lack of sleep and a schedule emerges (yes, it will actually happen), tackling the weight loss isn't as hard as it sounds. Simply adding a little exercise to your daily regimen and skipping a few of those bags of chips might just take the swing away from your jelly belly and put it back in your step. And squeezing your butt back into your old jeans for the first time can be practically orgasmic.

MOMINATRIX SAYS

Whether you're watching the pounds melt off or you've still got that tire around your waist, one of the best things you can do for yourself and your baby is to hydrate with water, especially if you're breastfeeding. It'll keep your supply up, and it will really help flush out toxins and extra water weight you might be carrying.

Breastfeeding the Pounds Away

Now many doctors, midwives, and lactation consultants will promote breastfeeding as a fantastic form of postpartum weight loss, when in actuality, it really depends on the person and not necessarily on whether you breastfeed or not. Breastfeeding does help in shrinking the uterus back down to size, which can help you appear less weighty, but many women do not experience rapid weight loss with breastfeeding. So, if you're breastfeeding and you are still carrying the pregnancy padding, you are not alone. In fact, you actually need a bit of extra fat so that you can adequately feed your kid. Once you wean, you'll find the weight drop off a bit quicker. However, you can engage in healthy exercise and eating programs to assist in the process as well.

When it comes to diet programs, many moms are advocates of Weight Watchers, which actually offers a specific program for postpartum and nursing moms. Plus, it works on a points system that focuses on healthy eating instead of deprivation. Keep in mind, however, that if you are breast-feeding, you need to maintain a higher caloric intake because you're feeding a child. So, make sure that if you decide to do some type of "diet" program, you are not depriving your-self and therefore depriving your baby.

Let's Get Physical

Once your doctor or midwife has given you the "go ahead" (and yes, when it comes to any exercise other than lifting and carrying your baby, you should get official approval), exercise can be the key to drop the rest of those pregnancy pounds and feel much better about yourself in general. Clearly fitting into a regular pair of pants, even if they are still a bit larger than your old ones, can be the key to turning on your sex button. And exercise will actually give you extra energy, which is always good for a romp in the sack.

MOMINATRIX **SAYS**

Starting an exercise program is a great excuse to buy some new shoes. Not only is it possible that your feet have changed since you had a baby, but it's important that you have the proper support while you're working out.

Exercising with a baby can create a bit of a challenge—or a big one if you've got a high-needs baby. In most cases, the last thing you'll feel like doing is squeezing in a walk on the treadmill or suffering through a few pushups. How-ever, there are a bunch of fantastic options for moms that might just give you the extra boost you need. And if you keep in mind that in the long scheme of things, exercise is a great way to get your energy levels up, it's definitely worth spending the few minutes each day increasing your heart rate.

Before you hit the pavement running or walking briskly, realize that there are some pregnancy body changes that will not be affected by exercise. The stretch marks, extra skin, and nonexistent butt are oftentimes par for the course. And no amount of exercise or dieting will shrink your feet back to their original size. But before you run off to your local plastic surgeon, it's definitely worth attempting a regular exercise program or regimen to see how your body responds.

Gyms

If you've got a bit of a budget to play with, a gym membership might be a great way to go. First, they may offer free child care, not only for your workout but also while you shower and get dressed. This could guarantee you a few moments of complete and utter peace, which will probably recoup the value of your monthly fee in terms of sanity alone.

Most gyms have long hours of operation, so you can easily coordinate your visits around naptime, and resources such as personal trainers and aerobics classes—or better, striptease classes—can help you maximize your workout and target train so you're not wasting your precious waking hours. And depending on the time of day that you go, you might be able to meet other moms, which is always a great way to pass time on the elliptical machine.

Mom-and-Baby Classes

One quick Google search or glance in your local phone book will lead you to find a plethora of local and national franchise mom-and-baby workout classes, with everything from stroller aerobics to baby yoga. Just make sure the classes are conveniently located and scheduled at a time that makes sense for you. Spending half your day driving togo to a thirty-minute baby yoga class probably isn't the best use of time.

Some moms, particularly those with finicky babies, might be hesitant to join these classes for the legitimate fear that their babies will scream the entire time and only exercise their patience rather than their thighs. In that case, take a trial class, play around with class times, and keep your expectations terribly low. While you may not get the workout that you were expecting, it is still a great way to get out of the house and commiserate with other moms, most of whom will be extremely understanding if your baby happens to wail for the entire class. And it's probably still more exercise than you were getting by checking the mail and mixing baby cereal all day.

MOMINATRIX **SAYS**

If you're at a loss for where to find mom-and-baby classes, try Stroller Strides *(www.strollerstrides.com)* or Baby Boot Camp *(www.babybootcamp.com)*, two well-known national exercise franchises that offer classes in most large and even moderately sized cities across the United States. And because these classes are in high demand, you can probably find a fair share at your local community center, YMCA, or gym.

Home Workouts

If a tight budget or wailing babies are a concern, then you can certainly make do in your own home. Thanks to a plethora of home workout resources, you'll have no problem finding anything from cool DVDs to books to huge, expensive elliptical machines (so much for budget, right?) that will help you create a workout program in your own home. And if you've got access to the Internet, you can even download an entire postpartum workout series right to your computer (*www.exercisetv.tv*).

It can be pretty tricky, however, to make time amidst the piles of laundry and the butt wiping to do a few sit-ups, and chances are, you might be pretty tempted to use your at-home yoga mat for a quick catnap. But with a bit of dedication and time management, you can certainly jump, dance, and even strip off the pregnancy pounds, whether baby is cooperative or not.

And if nothing else works, don't forget that sex actually burns calories.

MOMINATRIX SAYS

Jillian Michaels's 30-Day Shred *(www.jillianmichaels.com)* can get you back in shape in only twenty minutes a day, leaving you plenty of nap time left to get other stuff done.

NINE MONTHS ON, NINE MONTHS OFF

You'll have no shortage of people telling you that it took you nine months to gain the weight, so you've got to give yourself at least nine months to take it off. That doesn't mean it will make you feel any better when you still can't fit into your old pants, or the only hairstyle you have the energy for is bed head.

Still, the last thing you want to do is overwhelm yourself with unreasonable expectations. Remember, you're lugging around or chasing around a baby, so it's a given that you're going to have less time and energy. The best thing to do is pick one goal that's most important to you and go with it. Maybe it's losing ten pounds by a certain date, refusing to leave the house without makeup, or permanently retiring baseball hats as an appropriate fashion choice. While these might seem like small accomplishments, at this stage of the game, *small* is a relative term. Plus, when your days are often filled with more failures than successes, size really doesn't matter. Like anything else, re-sex-ify yourself in moderation. You might have become a mother overnight, but getting your groove back and finding a happy medium could take a little bit longer.

HELPING A
DADDY OUT

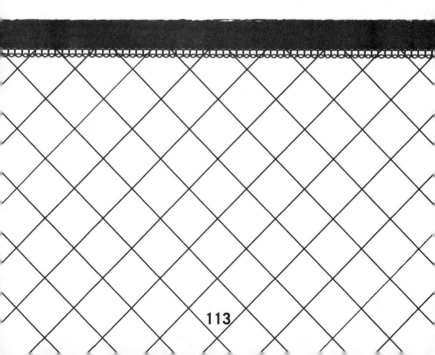

113

At this point in your parenting career, you certainly don't need to be reminded that it takes two to tango. And as you slowly graduate from maxi pads and oversized T-shirts back to the land of the living, you will probably find that your partner has some transitioning to do as well. Granted, he's already done his fair share of adjustment during your pregnancy. Most likely, he had to cope with all the lovely physical and emotional changes that affected your sex life, whether you had some sort of sexual awakening or didn't want to be touched by his seven-inch pole. Whether you realize it or not, his patience, fortitude, and overall tolerance have been stretched almost as much as your belly. And even though he may not have to tuck loose belly skin into his underpants, the ups and downs of being the pregnant partner can take its toll and impact what happens in your bedroom later on.

Since you're functioning on significantly fewer brain cells these days, it can be quite a challenge to find the time to use a separate shampoo and conditioner, let alone discuss the changes you've undergone courtesy of the new miniature member of your household. If you're like most parents out there, your relationship has taken a backseat to the baby, no matter how much you vowed it wouldn't.

But don't guilt yourself about losing touch with your partner. You're only human, after all, and so a few sacrifices on both your parts might be in order. And while toddlers, preschoolers, and even tweens are not necessarily easier than your wee one, their demands on your time are incredibly different.

When it comes down to it, your partner is an adult, for God's sake. He shouldn't require as much coddling and attention as your baby.

Even so, life might be inordinately easier if you could give him a set of crib notes and a trusty map to help him make his way through the early months as a new dad and postpartum partner. Unfortunately, you're not at liberty to take a night off to pen a paraphrased version of what's going on in your head, or the exact route to your G-spot.

So think of this chapter as a window into your post-partum mind. Take a minute to whip through it with a highlighter pen, and then pop this book in your significant other's "golf" magazine—you know, the one that he reads for the "interesting articles." Or leave it in his private reading library (aka the bathroom). It will get him up to snuff on what it's going to take to light your fire.

THE EMOTIONAL ROLLER COASTER

Men, if you think pregnancy was a bad amusement park ride, then the postpartum adventure is like a gigantic out-of-control roller coaster. And the strength of your stomach will directly determine how you make it through the first few months of parenthood, especially since you've got a tiny human being at the helm.

Parenting in the early months brings way too many unpredictable factors together in one big head-on collision, so it's best to keep your expectations at street level and just go with the flow. That means keeping your mind and your heart open to whatever the new mom and baby in your life need, along with being extra attentive, understanding, and well, father-like, because you're dealing with two people who can use all the caretaking they can get, no matter how much they think they can do it on their own.

MOMINATRIX SAYS

Okay, so maybe the whole open mind and heart thing isn't the manliest of duties, but there's really nothing manly about parenting, so best get over that now and get in touch with your feminine side.

By assisting in anything that you are physically equipped to do (sorry, but the breastfeeding might be tough), you're not only earning brownie points for future use, but you're ensuring that your partner and your kid will have the best start possible. And considering all the sacrifices your partner went through to get that little human being out so Junior could scream at you for hour-long intervals in the baby swing, you should consider yourself extremely lucky that all you have to do is wipe a tiny ass every few hours.

If there was ever a time that the woman is always right, it's now. And while desperation will most certainly get your ass in gear, you probably don't want to have to figure out how to use a bottle for the first time with no one around except one very pissed off and hungry baby. So be sure to request a few lessons from your partner—*now*. That doesn't mean you don't get to have a say on how to care for your baby. While maternal instincts definitely do kick in, your paternal ones will give you a swift kick in the *cojones* at some point in time, hopefully prior to your first session alone with your baby. Granted, they may not always do you that much good since you don't have boobs, but you should still listen to them just the same.

That being said, be super-careful about how you express those instincts. After all, you're not trying to one-up your partner or always be right; it's a team effort with your baby's health and happiness as the prize. So don't launch into some ridiculous "I told you so" dance if it turns out that you were the one who discovered that your baby is not eternally cranky but rather just going through a growth spurt. Better to let her believe that it was her own epiphany. The self-esteem boost will be most appreciated, particularly since she'll probably feel like a smacked ass for not figuring it out sooner.

But most of all, do your best to help her keep some semblance of her sanity. That means responding to her every beck and call with an uncanny attention to detail. If she wants half a glass of orange juice and half a glass of cranberry juice with a twist of lime, then for God's sake, do exactly that. She's a pinging ball of frazzle right now and the last thing you need is to exacerbate an already tenuous situation. It's just not about you, at least for the first few months (hopefully not years, but get ready), and you'll reap the most benefits overall if you figure that out really fast.

Whether or not you're tuned into that infamous "six-week recovery period" that doctors tout to couples as being a good indicator for when sexual intimacy can resume, whatever you do, do not bring it up. Along with incredibly sore nether regions, she's dealing with a whole slew of other important and more pressing issues, so the absolute last thing she needs is for you to ask her about sex.

That's right. *Do not ask her about sex.*

Instead tell her how great she's doing, how amazed you are at her ability as a mom, and how much you just plain old love her. Then go take a well-timed shower and exercise patience.

Keep your feelers out (metaphorical ones, boys) and get a sense of where she stands emotionally. Just because she doesn't want to do the nasty doesn't mean she couldn't use a little bit of lovin'. Just be clear on what her definition of "lovin'" entails.

Show your interest in subtle ways, like tucking her hair behind her ear, hugging her tightly, and kissing her gently, and allow her to be the barometer for ramping things up. No one said you can't engage in foreplay or other alternative sexual acts that do not involve you going near her vagina with anything other than an ice pack.

And if you get the sense she's just doing it for you, the poor sex-deprived partner who will spontaneously combust without sex, then you should really consider backing out, graciously of course. Chances are she needs sleep way more than you need a blowjob.

Inside Her Mind

If you could get inside the head of a postpartum mom, well, you'd probably want to jump right the hell back out again and go slug a few beers. Learning the ins and outs of a new human being and translating that information into something that keeps a baby alive is pretty damn taxing on an already tired brain. Toss in a fair share of feeling overwhelmed, doubtful, and possessed by raging hormones (can't forget those), and she's walking the fine line between sane and insane.

Regardless of whether she's a type A overachiever or a type B slacker, motherhood brings all women a startling feeling of incompetence that can be difficult to swallow. With most things in life, there are books, instruction guides, or classes, but with babies, it's just pure trial and error. You can sit and read as many books as you want, but there's no guarantee that they'll work for your kid.

Most good doctors and midwives will make sure to tell you about the "baby blues," a typical postpartum occurrence that involves a little more crying than you might usually see from your partner. Not surprisingly, women will have varying levels of the blues, not only due to raging hormones, but to how they deal with the adjustment that becoming a mother entails.

If you put everything that a woman experiences and sacrifices into perspective and juxtapose that with all that they have to deal with, it's not surprising that moms experience a blue period directly following birth. And it shouldn't surprise you that many moms experience more than just a few daily crying spells for the first few weeks.

Regardless of how your partner has dealt with pressure, anxiety, and challenging situations prior to having kids, the weight of a person's total existence on your shoulders is unlike anything else on this planet. So be tuned into what she's feeling and how the challenges are manifesting themselves.

MOMINATRIX **SAYS**

Postpartum depression is a serious condition and should not be taken lightly. Some signs include: feeling overwhelmed, feeling helpless, crying uncontrollably, experiencing thoughts of hurting herself and/or the baby, and depression. Don't hesitate to call a doctor. It's much better to be wrong than sorry.

Her Body

You probably simply adjusted to your partner's proud, pregnant body. But whether you loved it, liked it, or ran screaming from it, this new postpartum body can be a bit more difficult to welcome—not necessarily for you but certainly for your partner. You can gauge how tough it's going to be based on whether or not she pulled out all her pre-pregnancy clothes before you left for the hospital, or worse, packed her favorite before-baby jeans in her hospital overnight bag.

Generally speaking, it can take up to nine months (or more) for her body to go back to pre-pregnancy size, and even then, chances are high that she'll still have extra "this and that" hanging on even when all the weight is gone. When the baby came out she lost only Junior's weight plus a *bit* more—the rest will take time. Give your partner some support and gently remind her of this fact when she's trying to squish herself back into clothes that should clearly remain packed away for at least a few more weeks if not months.

Unfortunately, the postpartum body doesn't necessarily scream "sex," and therefore many moms are even more self-conscious than they might have been during their pregnancy. Their tummy is floppy, their butt is still pretty darn big, and their sore leaking boobs are more of a pain in the ass than an asset at this point in time.

The plus side is that having the baby is almost instantly liberating to the female body, so while she may not love her skin, at least she can now move freely in it. That may not be enough motivation to get her in the sack, but if you're able to work some magic, preferably in the pitch-black darkness, then she might be swayed based solely on the fact that she does not require a crane to move her between positions.

Of course, just because she's strategically tucking her belly into her pants doesn't mean that your partner can't still feel sexy. Nor does it mean that you can't make her feel sexy. It does, however, take specialized skills to sweet-talk someone who's not feeling so sweet. Your gentle, honest compliments can definitely work to your advantage when delivered effectively. However, if you've yet to master that fine art, you might just think about shutting your trap or changing the subject, particularly if you're feeling a bit taken aback by her physical appearance. Just remember that the rule still stands: Her butt does not look big in those jeans.

The Mominatrix's Guide to Conversational Post Partum-ese

Complaint: My pants don't fit.

Response: Eh well, I never liked you in pants anyway.

Complaint: I still feel gigantic.

Response: You always look thin on top of me.

Complaint: This ass has got to go.

Response: And I've got just the place for it.

Her Sex Drive

A dip in sex drive is usually most related to breastfeeding, but even if you're bottle-feeding your baby, her motivation for frolicking in the sack will be affected courtesy of that little but seemingly important human necessity called *sleep.* Truly, postpartum sex drives are a case-by-case phenomenon, and therefore, it's important to walk the fine line of expressing your sexual desire for your partner without pissing her off. Many men have a clear inability to bridge this wide gap, which means they often find themselves locked in the proverbial doghouse.

In particular, the breastfeeding mother is knee-deep in a hormone called *progesterone* that helps milk production but can limit moisture and sex drive. While some women can battle with their hormones and come out on top (in more ways than one), others are severely affected by this and have absolutely no sexual desire. Factor in the anxiety, resentment, and daily defeat that can often taint early motherhood, and you shouldn't be surprised if your partner wants nothing to do with you—other than to discuss what you can do to help make life easier. And if you could give her a few hours of peaceful, uninterrupted sleep, that might help too.

This does not, however, mean that you're in a completely hands-off situation. It just means that your hands might be doing something else at this point in time, perhaps with the baby instead of your partner. Make sure she knows how hot you think she is, but don't cross the line from supportive dad to sex-obsessed skeevo.

ANNOYING	APPRECIATED
Ass smack	Wiping baby's ass (and changing the diaper)
Boob grab	Bringing baby when Junior wants the boob
Request for sex	Asking if she needs help
Midnight molestation	Waking up at midnight to feed and change the baby

Once you make it back into the bedroom, you'll want to get a sense of who should take the reins. If you're feeling uncertain as to how fast to proceed, take your cues from her. If she's feeling fragile, uncomfortable, or frazzled, allowing her to take the lead might actually make her feel more in control of her life in general. However, since she's already busy caring for someone else twenty-four hours a day, maybe she'd actually appreciate it if you'd take over in the bedroom. For many women, being able to let go and allow someone else to take charge is a definite turn-on. Base your tactical approach on what she's saying and how she's acting. You just made it through nearly ten months with a pregnant woman, so trying to figure out what your partner wants in bed shouldn't be that difficult of a task. Besides, you can always ask for a few directions. And if you get it wrong, as you probably know quite well already, you'll hear about it.

ADJUSTMENTS

You've already changed your entire life around for this little baby, and now you're being asked to do more. With all the baby gear and clothes strewn about your house and the sleep schedule that has clearly gone on a permanent vacation, many parents hope that they can at least fall back on sex. And sure, it would be nice if just one thing, one very good thing, would stay exactly the same, but that's usually not the case. Even moms and dads who are completely unfazed by parenthood still have to make a few changes in the bedroom, even if it's just cutting the length of time in the sack or keeping the moans to a quiet whisper.

So do your best to take it in stride, because if it doesn't bother you to have to change a few things around, then there's a good chance your partner will be able to swallow it as well. Bitching about it will undoubtedly make it worse for both of you. Commiseration is fine, but whining is never allowed—from kids or from dads.

Since you've probably already made massive adjustments to almost every part of your daily existence, a few minor changes in the bedroom shouldn't be a huge deal. And remember, if making those changes translates into actually getting laid, it's probably worth the cost.

Clothes On

Whether or not your partner is feeling hugely confident about her floppy midsection, total and utter nakedness might not be the sexiest choice. Don't be surprised if she prefers to keep a few extra articles of clothing on during your lovemaking sessions. Her trusty T-shirt or tank top doesn't need to hinder your enjoyment of her body. See it as a challenge to get creative and make it part of the foreplay. Who knows? You might just get her to slip it off without even thinking twice.

Hands Off

The power of touch is an essential part to any intimate activity, but make sure you're rubbing and grabbing in the right places. Certain parts might be more sensitive than others, which could be a good thing or a bad thing. The battle wounds from having a baby, like c-section scars and hemorrhoids, can make moms uncharacteristically uncomfortable. And if your partner is breastfeeding, make sure you check in before offering up the boob love.

Positions

Until all body parts and nether regions have settled back into their rightful places, it's best to let your partner decide how she'd like to engage in intercourse. While you might like to toss her legs over her head and bang her to tomorrow, pass the reins and allow her to take charge. If she generally prefers male-dominant positions, you'll want to do those last. Ease her into them very slowly and check in to make sure the moans are actually from enjoyment and not from pain.

Lube It Up

You can expect to encounter dryness, so stock up on lube and be prepared with piles of hand towels—or, depending on where you are in parenthood, burp cloths and cloth diapers. Hell, you're going to wash them anyway, so you might as well not make extra work for yourself.

If your partner is breastfeeding, it's best to go with a water-based lube, like Astroglide (*www.astroglide.com*). And even if she's not, the water-based lubes will keep things slick, but you won't feel like you just rolled in an oil slick.

The Other Stuff

If actual sex is off the table, open up the nightstand drawers and be creative. Dig out the sex toys or any other paraphernalia that might get you both off without requiring you to actually be inside her. And remember, just because she might need a little extra help from a battery-operated toy doesn't mean she's ready to trade you in. Keep your eyes on the prize and realize that her enjoyment and comfort might be more important than your ego.

YOU CAN'T ALWAYS GET WHAT YOU WANT (OR MAYBE YOU CAN)

It shouldn't come as a surprise when sex starts to drop lower and lower on your list of things to do. By the time that you and your sex life are able to adjust to the new baby, you'll encounter a slew of new and exciting developments in your child that will make actually doing it pretty damn complicated, such as cutting teeth all night long. But if there's ever a time in your relationship when she needs you to be supportive, loving, and completely sane, it's now. Listen to her, talk with her, and just let her know that you're on her team, regardless of how clueless you might feel or actually be, and of how crazy she's acting.

Of course, you may also be contending with a bunch of hormonal issues that, for the most part, are completely out of your control. But don't give up. While pleading, begging, or taking cold showers may appear to be your only hope, it will probably take only a few strategic moves on your part to get her going—or, at least, to get her to a place where she will consider hopping on for a ride.

Presents

Never underestimate the power of well-timed gifts, which include—but are not limited to—flowers and jewelry. Do not buy your partner any type of clothing or lingerie item at this point in time, because failing to buy the correct size can completely jeopardize your entire plan. If you buy something too big, then it means you think she's a gigantic whale, which makes you a thoughtless asshole. And if you buy something too small, then you're obviously not in tune with what she's going through, and you're just trying to make her feel guilty about not working out. Did you really think she'd fit into that size "small" thong? Yes, buying clothes, lingerie, or undergarments of any kind should be knocked right off your list.

Many significant others are now being encouraged to purchase "push presents," which are supposed to represent their undying thanks to their partners for squeezing a human being from their crotch. She pushes out your off-spring; you buy her a present. Sounds completely logical, right?

Yes. To a dude.

Certainly the sentiment of a push present is deeply appreciated, but truly, the reward of getting the baby out of her body and onto her lap is payment enough. Gifts are always welcome, so there's no need to label them for a specific event. Besides, if you happen to buy her something cheap and shoddy as a push present, you're liable to never get laid again. And while a gigantic diamond might typically be a great way to say thanks, you're just not going to be able to buy anything to equal the pain that she went through to get that baby out. Even the freaking Hope Diamond would pale in comparison to her experience.

So a better approach is to surprise her every now and then with a simple, meaningful gift. Just make sure that what you are buying for her is actually considered a gift. That means absolutely no appliances, kitchen tools, or big-screen televisions, unless she has specifically requested them.

Chores

Watching a new dad vacuum or clean the dishes might just be the most powerful aphrodisiac out there. If you want a nearly guaranteed way to get some type of sexual favor, pick up a broom, mop, or some combination of both and clean. Do it without being asked and you might just get a little something extra.

It's important that when you're doing chores, you have a clear idea about how they should be completed. When it comes to housework, many women have a specific direction in which the floor should be mopped, or an order in which the shelves must be dusted, so diverting from these directives could result in adverse effects. And while you think your partner might just be too exhausted to care, think again. Remember this mantra when it comes to cleaning: *Never mess with the system.* And here's one when it comes to grocery shopping: *Never fuck with the list.* The specific steps and items that are part of her systems and lists are there for a reason. Learn these well before you pull out your bucket or attempt to tackle the grocery store.

MOMINATRIX SAYS

Comments like "Wow, this is such a hard job" or "Honey, I just don't know how you do this!" in an appreciative and sincere tone can go a long way. It's those extra touches that could mean the difference between a hand job and a blowjob.

A good rule of thumb is to start with something that she's always begging you to do as opposed to something that she generally does. Maybe leave the towel folding and closet organization to her and take this opportunity to pick up your underwear and move them two more feet into the laundry basket, or empty all the fourteen-year-old dress shirts from the closet into a donation bin. She'll be happy that you finally heeded her dire requests.

Once you've tackled old requests, try doing some household chores. It's important to remember that even if it's a small, simple task, *never ever* suggest that you are, in fact, better or more competent at it. It's tough out there for a mom these days, and with everyone seemingly judging her decisions, the last thing she needs is to feel judged by you at home. Repeat after me: *She* is the expert at scrubbing toilets—or at everything that involves cleaning, for that matter. Besides, if you decide to brag just a little too much about your housekeeping abilities, you're asking for those to be tacked onto your duty list. So, keep your mouth shut and save your bragging for the bedroom.

Sitter

Depending on how old your new addition is, you might consider finding a babysitter to watch Junior so you can get out as a couple. This can be an incredibly tricky situation, but one that will reap great rewards if you follow these instructions extremely carefully.

Unless you've got relatives close by, most moms are pretty hesitant to leave their baby with random babysitters, even if you've done forty background checks and cleared their references. So if you've got a newborn, it's probably best to just let your partner go out on her own for a few hours (or less if she's breastfeeding) while you take care of the baby. Okay, so maybe that just freaked you out, but there's actually very little that can go wrong (other than the baby screaming for the entire time that she's gone). And while you might feel like an incredibly big smacked ass if that happens, it's really not the worst thing in the world.

Hopefully, you've been proving your worth in diaper changes and baby bouncing over the last few weeks, so your partner will not freak out at the prospect of leaving the child with you. If you get the sense that she fears you will be unable to handle the situation on your own, then by all means don't suggest it. But if you're feeling confident and she's expressed an interest in getting out, then telling her to go get a manicure or pedicure on her own will be a huge turn-on.

Just make sure not to call her while she's gone. And when she returns, be honest—if the baby did scream, tell her that, but then follow it up with the fact that you were both fine. If you call her repeatedly or toss the baby at her the second she walks in the door, she will be less inclined to go out or do anything on her own for a very long time.

Once you're both feeling comfortable leaving the baby, it's a great time to book a sitter (or family member) for a couple of hours so you can get out together. The key is that YOU are the one who is taking the initiative in setting up the sitter. Consider going out for breakfast or lunch (instead of dinner), mainly because babies often do better and have a bit more of a regular schedule during the day. However, if you've got a kid who sleeps for a few-plus hours in a row at night, then go out later and grab a snack and a drink at the bar. Once you get a sense of your babe's schedule, then you'll know what will be the best time to tackle a "date."

Finding a reliable sitter can be a huge challenge. Make sure that you set up someone whom your partner knows well and you've used before. If you don't have a regular sitter, talk with your partner about finding someone. Showing that you're interested in taking her out and being with her—not because you're sick of the baby, but because you think it'll be fun and a nice change of scenery—can be incredibly hot. Most moms will want to have a hand in picking the babysitter, so if you can't set one up without her knowing, at least put the bug in her ear, or ask your neighbors and friends for some recommendations so that the search isn't as difficult and time-consuming.

MOMINATRIX SAYS

Online sitter services, like *www.sittercity.com* and *www.care.com*, are a great way to find a sitter. For a nominal membership fee, you can search for sitters by Zip Code, and do everything from checking personal and professional references to viewing an official background check. And always make sure to pay your sitters well and leave good snacks; it's insurance that you won't lose them to another family.

If you've already got a nanny or relative who is watching your little one or has done so on occasion, then you will impress the crap out of your partner by booking that person in advance and setting up every little detail of the actual date. This way, you can usher her right out of the door and into the car when the sitter arrives, instead of spending half of the evening trying to figure out where to go and what to do. You may only have a short window of time to get out, so make your preparations ahead of time. You'll get to spend much more quality time together, and you might even have a little left over to fool around on the way home.

Job Swapping

Depending on what your typical duties are around the house, you should strongly consider swapping jobs with your partner at various times during the day. If you're planting your ass on the couch every night or off playing golf on the weekends, then this is going to be a hard adjustment (and ps: *shame on you*). But even if you're an active dad and partner, taking on duties that aren't necessarily yours can afford you a direct ticket right into your partner's pants.

The concept of job swapping is simple: Do something that you don't usually do without being asked or told. Offering to make dinner one night during the week, or putting the kids to bed on a night that is not designated as yours, will definitely get noticed. If she's always the one doing the grocery shopping, volunteer to take her list (and the kids) and do it for her.

Of course, if you're dealing with a super mom, then it's important to pick your jobs wisely. Certain moms are more willing to let go and let someone else do things, while others tend to like to have their little finger in everything. So, if she doesn't care how the dishes are washed, then that's the job to snag. If she's got strong opinions as to how the grocery shopping is supposed to be done, then you may want to skip over that one, or do your best not to disappoint. For the most part, doing a little extra around the house and playing Mr. Mom without having a honey-do list waved in front of your face can be the fast track right to bedroom bliss.

SOLID AS A ROCK

Truthfully, during the first twelve months—or longer—sex will be the least of your worries, thanks to the new addition in your household. Many couples report that along with lack of sleep and energy, the first year of parenting puts a huge strain on a relationship.

With all the ups and downs that come with having a baby, moms tend to put a lot of pressure on themselves, partly due to human nature, and partly due to how society views moms, to do it all. It's tough out there for a mom these days, and with everyone seemingly judging her decisions, the last thing she needs is to feel judged at home.

If there's a time in your relationship where she needs you to be supportive, loving, and completely sane, it's now. Listen to her, talk with her, and just let her know that you're on her team, regardless of how clueless you might feel or actually be and how crazy she's acting.

You're not a babysitter or live-in help. You are her partner and co-parent in this new adventure, and while you might not be able to physically do as much as she does with the baby right now, your time will come. Oh yes it will. For now, your presence and partnership is what she needs most.

No matter how much sex you were or are having, if you let your relationship go down the tubes, not only will you eventually suffer, but your kids will too. So treat your partner like a goddess and be present for your family. There's really just nothing sexier than that.

7

SINGLE MOMS NEED HOT SEX TOO

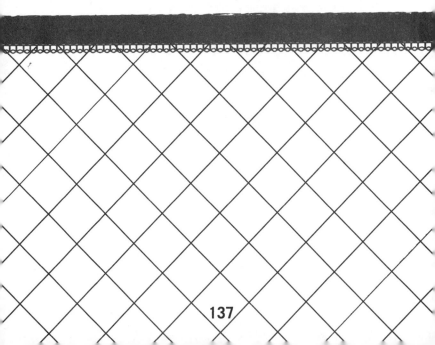

Ah. Where to find a man? This is the plight of many single moms everywhere. Well, that and where the hell to find a reliable babysitter. Long before kids were even a twinkle in your eye, finding guys was a no-brainer. In fact, you probably had to turn down hordes of eligible keg-diving frat boys at one point in your life. But when the only boys at your fingertips are your own sons, you might find yourself wondering what the hell happened to all the men. Suddenly, you may find yourself not so focused on pecs and penis size, but rather on whether the guy has got a fairly steady income and is responsible enough to be a parent to your kids. (Okay, so maybe you still care about penis size, but it takes you a bit longer to make that determination.)

As a single mom, you'll probably find that one-night stands are a thing of the past—not so much because you just aren't into that sort of thing anymore, but because trying to explain why the heck some stranger is flipping pancakes in your kitchen in your bathrobe is way too complicated to explain to your kids.

Personal chef? Um, nice try.

And don't worry that baggage from your previous relationship will ruin your chances. You can toss those suitcases full of unresolved issues and codependency right in the trunk, because now you've got a kid or two to worry about. And regardless of their size, the weight of your kids' livelihood and well-being is way heavier than anything else you might be bringing into another relationship.

But no matter how you arrived at singlehood, there's one thing that rings true when it comes to being a mom on her own: It's pretty damn hard.

So while your desire to meet men and enjoy a social life outside of kid-centered activities is warranted, finding the time as well as the venue to meet men who are not single due to imprisonment is extremely difficult. And you can forget about that constant "It'll happen when you least expect it" bullshit that every single person in the world wants to shove back into the mouth of every married person who says it.

Point blank, finding available men as a single woman— let alone as a mother—is a tough task. You're probably spending countless hours at work, where you don't want to date anyone. Then, during the extra time that's left over, you like to be with your kids. So really, that leaves you just enough time to hire an escort for a quickie in the backseat of your car while it's parked in your garage. And really, who has the money for escorts these days?

THE UPS AND DOWNS OF SINGLE PARENTHOOD

Believe it or not, there are some benefits to single parenting. Sure, an extra household salary would be a plus, but this way you aren't bickering with someone about diaper changes, time away from the kids, or household chores. And while it's always nice to have an extra set of hands, when you don't need to discuss things with a partner, it's a lot easier to manage the enormous number of decisions you have to make just to get through an ordinary day. Listen, even those couples with harmonious marriages have secretly considered taking up the single life just so they could do things their own way. Being married is difficult, but adding children completely complicates matters. So enjoy the fact that you can do things on your own, the way you want to do them, without having to ask, check, or double-check with someone else.

Of course, making everyday decisions is only a small part of the challenging role that single moms play. Being both parents to your kids can certainly take its toll. And when you add in work and everything else that comes with running a household, doing it all on your own often leaves very little time for you to spend with your own kids, let alone by yourself.

A GOOD MAN IS HARD TO FIND

You might think that all the good men are either married or bitter, courtesy of the 50 percent divorce rate in our country. And in some cases, you're probably right. But much to your advantage, men are marrying later in life. And there are still plenty of them who have not been irrevocably damaged by their evil first wife. Who knows? Maybe they started out as assholes and a first marriage whipped them right back into reality. Regardless of how these guys found singledom, you should know that they're out there, and many of them are ready and waiting to be discovered by you.

Now, finding a man is sort of like shoe shopping. If you're looking for a great pair of shoes, you could go to one of those gigantic warehouses where you might get lucky on a very good day. However, remember that if you take this route, you will probably end up doing one of the following:

1. You will buy a pair of shoes you don't need and really shouldn't have taken off the sale rack—but you just couldn't help yourself.
2. You will grab a couple of pairs that aren't exactly what you're looking for but will do while you continue your search for the ultimate pair of shoes.
3. You will spend way too much time looking at shitty shoes and then get so frustrated you give up entirely.

You're probably better off hitting Bloomingdales, where you can score fairly easily without having to try on a bunch of crap that you'd probably never even think about buying in the first place. And since the shoes are so damn expensive, you're not likely to waste money on a pair you don't really *really* like. Get it? Good.

Where the Wild Men Are

So where the hell are the "Bloomingdales" of single, responsible hot men who are interested and willing to date a single mom and her kids? In order to find these men, you might have to actually go where they hang out.

Don't get too excited. You probably won't be able to get into the Yankees' locker room. And really, who wants to look at a bunch of sweaty dudes in jockstraps anyway?

If you're seeking out single or divorced dads, they might have just about as much time to meet women as you do to meet men. But then, many dads do not have full custody and therefore might have more time than a single mom to go out, although they might not go out on weekends, since that's often when they will have their kids.

MOMINATRIX SAYS

Don't be disappointed if you find the men but there's no match. Just getting out there and meeting people can get the ball rolling. While you may not hit it off with the people you meet, chances are they've got friends and family—and they have friends and family. You just never know what one chance meeting could turn into.

Phew. That's complicated. As you can see, you can analyze mating habits of single men like a zoologist in the jungle until you're blue in the face, but when it comes down to it, you'll have to rely on generalized tendencies, behavioral patterns, and good old-fashioned luck.

Sure, you could dress yourself up like a piece of meat and throw yourself to the proverbial wolves, but that's probably not going to get you the long-term results you are hoping for, unless you're on the prowl for a questionable reputation. So instead of trying to play treasure hunter with a cryptic map and an outdated sonar machine, get a sitter, grab a single female friend, a married girlfriend, or even a cool couple to go out with you and explore different male venues—basically, places where the single menfolk congregate.

Now that's pretty wide open for interpretation, so use what's left of your poor, tired single-mom brain and decide what makes sense. Spending time perusing the golf section at Dick's or casing the television section of Best Buy does not. And make sure to pick a place where you'll actually be the center of attention. You don't want to have to compete with a half-naked woman hanging precariously from a pole by her cellulite-free thighs, or worse, a bunch of football players tackling each other on a big screen.

Many women loathe the bar scene, which is what many brilliant married people will suggest you try. And while you can actually meet some great guys at a bar, as you might have guessed, you'll want to pick the bar or club pretty carefully. Places known for their one-dollar pitcher nights should not be anywhere on your list.

If the idea of bar and club hopping doesn't appeal to you, think about joining clubs or groups that are based on an interest in a particular activity. Of course, you must realize that the type of club or group you choose will tend to define its members. That doesn't mean you should necessarily stereotype people based on their interests, but if you're looking for a hot, hunky athlete, you probably don't want to join a chess club. *Sorry, chess players.*

If that's not appealing, you'll generally run the gamut of "types" at your local gym or community center. You might even start attending your local church or synagogue. You never know what a little Divine intervention might do.

But whatever activity you select, just make sure it's something in which you've got a genuine interest. While it might be great to date a cycling enthusiast, if you really hate riding bikes, the relationship probably won't go anywhere.

The Mominatrix's Three Unexpected Places to Meet Good Men

1. *Church.* Whether you're a religious type or haven't even thought about praying in years, joining a church community can be a wonderful way to meet good men. While you should never feel as though you need to compromise your values, many churches offer various singles groups, Bible study groups, and other meet-ups, and they often provide helpful support systems for families in need. And if you're chasing around a couple of kids on your own, then you're definitely in need.

2. *School events.* If your kids aren't school-aged yet, you might be shit out of luck, but when they start getting involved in extracurricular activities, sports, and other school-related events, make a point to join in. You might just meet a slew of single dads who have rightfully been put on kid duty during the evenings and weekends. Plus, you won't have to worry about "the big reveal," since it'll be pretty damn obvious that you have kids.

3. *Facebook.* This online meeting place, which was started by a Harvard college student, has now become

the way to connect with new and old friends, family, and everyone in between. While some users complain that it's a veritable collision of many worlds—babysitters, exes, and neighborhood friends—it's a great way to rekindle friendships and relationships with folks with whom you might have lost touch.

The Setup

Before you roll your eyes and start picturing a blind date that ends in ruins, remember that getting set up on a date by a friend, family, or even a coworker isn't the worst thing in the world, so long as you're careful to set specific parameters beforehand. And while many folks might have to dig deep to find a single guy friend for you, it's worth a try. Sometimes just letting people know that you're interested in dating is the first step. While it might seem obvious that you'd prefer not to sit alone folding socks and watching infomercials on a Saturday night, you'd be surprised at how clueless some people can be. Put the word out on the street that you're on the prowl.

MOMINATRIX SAYS

There's a difference between compromising who you are and stepping out of your comfort zone. Don't force yourself to go somewhere or join some group just so you can meet a guy. But if you might just enjoy it anyway, regardless of whether there's a potential for love and romance involved, then go for it.

The key to making the setup work in your favor and not turn into an awkward friendship-ending situation with the person who introduced you is to be clear about what you're looking for. While your friends and relatives might think they know you, it's best to make sure they understand your taste in men before they hook you up with someone you'd never even consider going out with in the first place. Just because the guy is "single" does not make him dating material. Let everyone know the type of guys you're interested in, and don't be shy about exchanging photos before they even attempt to set you up. This is a visually driven society, after all, and while you might not need the guy to look like Brad Pitt, you don't want Chewbacca—loyal to the Force or not—showing up at your front door.

MOMINATRIX SAYS

When you're single, any public "appearance" could be an opportunity to meet someone. Since you just never know who you're going to run into, always look your best. (Or as good as you can as an extremely busy, single working mom!)

So institute a "prescreening" or a meeting before you actually get set up on a date, either by "accident" or in some type of group situation (drinks after work, a party at a friend's house, you get the picture). That way, you will get a sense of who this person is before you pay a babysitter and dig out your date clothes. No one really has time to waste on a bad date, but especially when you're spending money and time away from your kids, you'll want to get a good sense of what you're getting yourself into before you take the plunge.

Online Dating

While it might seem odd to pay for a dating service, countless single moms have met amazing men via online dating. Depending on your budget, you'll find a variety of services that allow you to search for compatible singles by age, appearance, height, location, job, and maybe even personality; penis size and longevity probably aren't options, or at least ones listed in the official profile.

With so many online dating options out there, you might find it difficult narrowing down which one to pick. You can definitely categorize the services in a "you pay for what you get" type of manner. Many moms avoid the free sites, hoping that if you have to actually pay a fee to meet someone, you're going to find serious daters rather than dudes looking to score. But free doesn't necessarily mean bad, by the way, so if you're on a tight budget, then ask around for a few recommendations and join. Just be sure that your information is kept private, and consider setting up a separate e-mail address to use for dating purposes only. There's nothing wrong with using just your first name, and using a close, large city as your locale instead of your exact address.

Unfortunately, online dating is a crapshoot. You never know if the dude's picture is from five years ago and he's since lost all of his hair and packed on fifteen pounds. And while you might have great conversations over e-mail or even the phone, sometimes there's a reason people stick to online dating: They don't actually do well in real life.

This decoder will help you read through the lines on the dating profiles:

PROFILE DESCRIPTION	WHAT IT REALLY MEANS
Frugal	Cheap bastard
In touch with feminine side	Gay
Average build	Beer gut
Outgoing	Never shuts up
Young at heart	Older than your grandpop

For every not-so-great experience and horror story, you'll find one that ends in love, marriage, and babies, so if you're limited in time, energy, and opportunity, the world of online dating can certainly open up access to men whom you might never have gotten a chance to meet.

Regardless of which one you choose, using an online dating service can feel like jumping into a freezing cold ocean full of fish—and sometimes sharks—so it's important to complete your profile carefully. You'll also want to set up parameters for your own searches, including everything from location to common interests and whatever else you deem as important. Some people might say that beggars can't be choosers, but you're not trying to scrape up a few bucks to buy a box of cigarettes. You're trying to make a match with a potential mate. So instead of just casting a line, waiting to see who bites, and sifting through a ton of responses, you should limit your profile to what you deem as essential to your relationship and then leave out what you feel doesn't really matter one way or the other. And think hard about your parameters. If you're adamant on dating someone with blond hair, you're going to automatically rule out a group of possibly fantastic potential suitors. And really, there's a decent chance he won't have that hair forever, so stick with qualities that are definite deal breakers and be a little more flexible on things that can be changed or pulled out.

The Mominatrix's Top Three Online Dating Services

1. *Yahoo! Personals*. Search for singles based on your Zip Code, and send a free "icebreaker" to someone who tweaks your interest.
2. *Match.com.* You'll be able to peruse possible dates and up to twenty-six photos based on a specific list of preferences, and then contact them using an anonymous e-mail network.
3. *eHarmony.* Once you make it through the extensive prescreening questionnaire, you'll find potential partners who fit within the parameters of your results.

PICKY, PICKY, PICKY

No one is saying that you weren't picky before, of course, but when you add kids into the mix, dating becomes somewhat of an art and less like playing a few rounds of Russian roulette. Once you've found a few guys, or even just one, whom you're interested in grabbing a drink with, you've got to deal with more factors than whether or not you have chemistry. It's one thing if you get along famously with your date, but the real question is whether he'll get along just as famously with your child.

Many single moms make the decision to seperate their dating self from their parenting self, adding the kids in later on like their special bonus deal. *Surprise! I have a kids. You've just won the lottery!* The only problem is that for some men, kids are not necessarily seen as bonuses, and so all the time you might have spent getting to know him could be completely for naught if he hits the highway once he finds out there's more than just you in the picture.

Some single moms might feel as though it's no one's business as to whether they have a kid or not. You don't know this guy from Adam, and so you're not obligated to tell them anything about you. You're just getting to know each other, and all that ancillary information, like you're a mom with kids (hello!) can wait.

MOMINATRIX SAYS

Tell him you're a mom with your words, not your appearance. That means tossing the mom uniform and ponytail and spiffing yourself up. You're a hot, single woman who happens to have kids. While you might not want to sport a miniskirt and halter top, you can certainly dress with sexiness and sophistication in mind.

Actually, in this scenario, you're just doing a fantastic job of covering up your fear that the guy will take off at the brief mention of the words "my kids"—either because you've seen your single-mom friends left in the dust, or it's already happened to you a few times. You're probably sick of hearing how they probably weren't worth your energy anyway. But in truth, you can't blame them for being a little shocked at the news, particularly if you had been dating for a while and then suddenly decided to share it casually over dinner.

No matter how afraid you are of rejection, don't let it keep you mum about your kids. In fact, it should motivate you to make it part of your dating profile or opening remarks. If he's getting you, he's getting your kids. You might as well start your new relationship with openness and honesty. You've got nothing to lose and your precious time won't be wasted. And if he's already got kids, your revelation might make him feel better about sharing his own family with you. Brady Bunch, eat your heart out.

REACTIONS TO THE BIG REVEAL

Whenever or however you decide to tell your boyfriend about your kids, be prepared for a few reactions. Thanks to the Internet and the telephone, you might not even need to tell him in person.

- *The Pretender.* He's the guy who lives in a fantasyland where he acts like he's dating a woman with no kids. Except you do have kids. *Move along.*
- *The Weirdo.* He'll embrace your child as his own and offer to buy you a gigantic house where all three of you can live happily ever, all on the first date. *Run.*

- *The Ignoramus.* This guy accepts the fact that you have a kid, but then wants absolutely nothing to do with Junior. *Good-bye.*
- *The Holder of Secrets.* He'll respond to your disclosure by telling you one of his very own, except and there's a good chance it's not something you want to hear. *Time to go.*

While being a parent might not be the first thing you want to discuss on your date, it's certainly not something you want to "accidentally" leave out. You spent plenty of years trying to transition from woman to mom; you don't want to attempt to separate that out. Being a mother is part of who you are, and it is something that should attract a guy to you, not scare him away. And more important, your job as a mom is going to come first. It's best to get that out in the open so that your date—and potential boyfriend—understands your priorities and limitations. You may not be available as often as he likes, and you might have to cancel dates without notice.

You'll also need to make it clear that establishing a dating relationship doesn't mean you will suddenly turn your life into a free-for-all. He'll need to understand that sleepovers will be few and far between because you just don't want to chance your kids seeing anyone's naked butt.

So whatever rules you might have had about dating before kids have changed. And if they haven't yet, then you should strongly consider making a few adjustments to what you're looking for in a guy. You're not just looking for a compatible mate. You're looking for someone who is worthy enough to be a father figure for your kids.

Here's a handy comparison chart to help you figure out if the dude is date or dad material:

THE SINGLE MOM'S DATE-WORTHY QUALITY CHECKLIST	
DATE	**DAD**
Nice car	Knows how to buckle a car seat
Sense of style	Dresses your kids in matching clothes
Smells great	Sniffs out baby poop
Treats you like a princess	Names all of the Disney princesses

But before you run out and try to find the most eligible dad for your kids, don't forget that you have needs too. So whoever you decide to date should be someone whom you like. Sure, it's great to find a guy who's totally into your kids. Heck, you might even find that downright sexy. But when that wears off, and your kids are grown and gone, are you going to look at this guy and wonder what the hell you were thinking?

SETTING THE EXAMPLE

As if finding a guy isn't hard enough, you've got a pair (or more) of little eyes watching your every move. You're already on your guard about what you say and how you act, knowing that your example is what your kids will learn from. So it shouldn't be a surprise that they'll be keeping their eye on how you go about your dating relationships from start to finish. And you can bet they won't be turning the channel to check out something more interesting.

Modeling a loving, respectful relationship for your kids is part of every parent's job, whether they will remember it or not. Sure, you can tell yourself that setting a good relationship example doesn't really matter when they're teeny tiny babies, and maybe it's true. Most likely, they won't remember hearing you scream at the top of your lungs. *Thank goodness for that.*

But as they get older, they will see how you interact with potential partners, and they'll store it back into their little spongy brains for future reference. So if you want your kids to make good choices about dating and love, you've got to show them how it's done by doing it for yourself. Your example will go way farther than your words—especially when you're dealing with a teenager who already thinks you're stupid.

Of course, all this is easier said than done, because much of dating is trial and error, but demanding respect should come naturally. If you're willing to put up with crap—whether it's small things like being a control freak or big things like name calling—then your kids are going to learn that tolerating or partaking in this sort of behavior is okay. But if you show them that you don't put up with any shit, you can bet that they'll adopt similar values. Or, at least, you can certainly hope.

ADAPTING TO BEING A PAIR

Once you've actually found a suitable guy and have entered into a dating relationship, you might find it hard to adjust to being part of a couple again. Let's face it. Regardless of how long you've been single, you've figured out a way to manage on your own, and so adding someone else into your life might require a bit of rearranging, not just in how you approach your own personal life, but in how you go about parenting as well.

Unless you've established a pretty fair co-parenting relationship with your ex (if he's even still in the picture), you've probably come to do most everything on your own.

Granted, there are dads who buy their kids clothes and take them to doctor visits, but for the most part, that stuff falls on the mom. You're the one making appointments and dropping them off at school. So allowing someone else to participate with you or—*gasp*—do it for you might actually make your toes curl. However, while it's great for your kids to see a super-capable and independent mom, it's also important for them to see someone who's willing to delegate duties and ask for help.

So you're obviously not going to let your new boyfriend discipline your kids, but he can certainly make a peanut butter and jelly sandwich and eat lunch with them. In getting to know you, he's going to have to get to know your kids, and part of that process might mean allowing him to do some of the things that would typically be on your plate. You're a family, after all, and in dating you, he's entering into an already formed system.

So decide what you're willing to let go of, and what duties your child will feel comfortable letting him do. He might be happy to take your toddler to the potty or get your preschooler dressed, but your kids might not yet be comfortable allowing him to do that. Find something you all agree on. Then do your best to just let go.

THE MOMINATRIX'S RECOMMENDED "EASE HIM IN" PARENTING DUTIES	
HOW TO KEEP HIM	**HOW TO DITCH HIM**
Feeding a happy baby at home	Feeding a hungry baby at a restaurant
Putting them to bed at bedtime	Putting them back to bed at 1 A.M., 3 A.M., 5 A.M.
Changing a pee-pee diaper	Changing a poo-nami
Taking them to the park	Taking them on a road trip
Wiping a sniffly nose	Removing a snail's trail of long green boogers

But whether you let him fold your towels or make him the designated dish washer, you might find that being a pair again is a little more challenging than you might have expected. You'll just have to decide what can be left for personal interpretation, and what absolutely, positively must be done by you.

Once you're able to let go and let someone else take over for a little while (or just join in on the adventure if you're a control freak), you'll hopefully be able to recognize the benefit of being together with someone else. (Well, aside from the regular sex.) Part of being in a relationship is that you're able to share duties with someone else.

When it comes down to it, becoming a pair should make your life easier, not harder. Sure, it'll take some time to adjust, but if you find yourself hating life more with your new partner than you did before, you might want to do some timely re-evaluation.

And while an optimistic attitude can be the key to happy, successful dating, for God's sake, never settle. If you are able to manage your life in its current situation regardless of how pretty or scary you make it look, you want someone who's going to complement that and make your life even better. Plus with the scores of fantastic — almost lifelike — dildos they're making now, you might just be better off buying a few batteries, hiring a babysitter, and enjoying a quiet evening all by yourself.

Just be better off buying a few batteries, hiring a babysitter, and enjoying a quiet evening all by yourself.

KEEPING THE
LOVE ALIVE

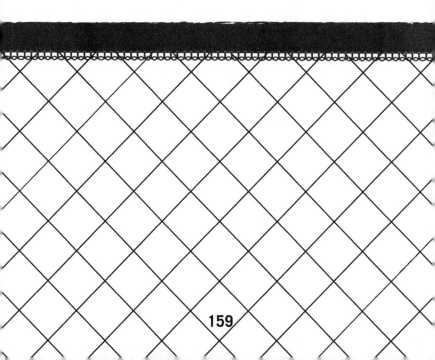

Inevitably, the wee babes who turn your sex life upside down and your body parts inside out grow up. Actually, by the time you get a chance to read this chapter, your kid might be already walking around.

Like everyone and their third cousin has probably told you, time flies, and now you're probably dealing with a toddler or a preschooler. Surprise! Toddler Junior is just as tyrannical as Baby Junior—except now there are words and opinions and tantrums in really public places.

But on the flip side, Toddler Junior is sleeping (hopefully) and eating from something that can't be confused for your boob, so you're willing to compromise. And best of all, you've packed away the banded pants and nursing bras for real clothes. *It's good to be alive, isn't it?*

So in theory, you should be extremely well rested and ready to hop in the sack at the drop of a teeny toddler baseball cap. *Right?* Wrong!

Instead, you're running the kid to bilingual music class and baby gym, and doing five thousand other things that are now so much easier since you don't have to lug a drooling baby along with you to do them. Holy sweet freedom! Only problem is that you're just as tired as you were before you were officially not getting sleep. And now it's not a screaming baby keeping you from doing the deed, but rather a quickly growing toddler who keeps you on your toes for more hours than you thought humanly possible. So when you've been stuck for who knows how many hours a day being bugged, badgered, and bothered by little hands grabbing at you from every direction, chances are high that the last thing you want is to be groped by your well-meaning partner.

What is it about the dad-species that makes them seem to believe that any woman, particularly when she just spent a large part of the day staring at her own kid's butt, would want them to grab hers? Perhaps you should be flattered that he thinks your tired, Cheerio-crumb-covered ass, draped in pants that could grab back on their very own, is groping material. Part of you might want to be treated like nothing ever changed—like you're still the young hot thing who could stand on her head during sex and give four-hour blowjobs. But then there's this other part of you that knows things are most certainly not the same. And quite frankly, there's absolutely nothing wrong with acknowledging it. Actually, most women do; it's oftentimes the partners who are still in denial.

Maybe they think you don't want to be treated any differently—that you want to know that your stretch-marked bellies still give them the same erection that your mostly taut stomachs did just a few years back. No woman really wants to hear that her body just isn't as attractive to her partner anymore. But most women know that the postpartum body isn't going to have the same "wow" effect that their body might have had prior to life with kids. Hell, you've probably given yourself a little scare staring into a mirror and wondering who the hell that person is who's glaring back at you.

The truth is, it's not just your body that has changed. Your sexual needs have too. When you've been through the childbearing ringer and are being used as a toddler jungle gym, you need the un-mommified parts to be acknowledged and touched. It's wonderful for him to cup your face in his hand, to stroke your soft (though perhaps greasy) hair, or put his arm around your waist. And nothing is hotter than when he reaches out to hold your hand while you are both sitting on the couch or kisses you softly while you're lying in bed.

And while that's not to say you don't enjoy being treated as the sexual being that you are—and always will be—sometimes a tender touch and a soft subtle stroke are exactly what will turn you on and make you believe, if only for a moment, that your flapping arms and saddle-bags are just a figment of your imagination.

GETTING BACK TO THE BASICS

Having a baby can definitely send even the most connected couples into a freaky, alternate universe, where baby toys engulf your entire living room and your evenings are spent rummaging through gigantic piles of laundry. With your time and attention aimed at a baby, it's not hard to lose touch with your partner. In fact, it's probably pretty darn normal. But if you put off your relationship in exchange for parenthood, then you might be in for a rude awakening when you decide you're ready to trade in those booties for some actual booty.

While your partner could probably do it with a corpse in the room at this point in time, you might not be able to hop right back into the sack cold turkey. And even if you have been sneaking in the weekly or biweekly sexual encounter, that's probably still all it is. And even that's just not going to be enough to get you through this ridiculously rocky ride. Acting as each other's occasional fuck buddy can be immediately gratifying, but in the long run, you're going to need to spend time together doing more than getting each other off. And discussing your kid's adorable antics and amazingly talented scribble drawings via e-mail and text messages does not count.

MOMINATRIX **SAYS**

Start a babysitting co-op in your neighborhood. Each week you alternate watching each other's kids. To make it easier, just make sure your kids are in bed before the neighbor arrives. You can enjoy the peace and quiet of someone else's house, along with free babysitting twice a month.

After all, you're in this parenting gig together, and the more you can support each other and connect on a more intimate level, the better the outcome will be for your kids and your sex life. Maybe childbirth and babydom have taken some of the wind out of your sails, but rest assured that love can actually conquer all. Even potty training.

Date Night

So the term "date night" has definitely gotten a bad rap, but before you roll your eyes, its original purpose should not be negated. Spending time together without the kids is essential to your relationship and your sex life. And if that's not motivating enough for you, it will give you a good reason to pull those sexy stilettos and tight dress out of the depths of your closet.

While it might have been quite a challenge to make couple's time Z other than that you can't find a reliable babysitter.

Babysitters really aren't that hard to come by, so long as you know how to find them and keep them coming back. If your kids are little rabid trolls, then you may be shit out of luck unless you've got a grandparent nearby. But if you've got a few tricks up your sleeve, then it probably won't even matter how crazy your kids are.

THE MOMINATRIX'S GUIDE TO KEEPING A BABYSITTER

- *Have good snacks.* A well-fed sitter is a happy one. If you're leaving the house with a few bags of Goldfish and some applesauce in your pantry, then you might as well just cross yourselves off her list. Buy a few things that you might not ever purchase and hide them in your "babysitter only" box until you've got a scheduled night out. Or better yet, make it a pizza night. Your kids won't even care that you're leaving, and your babysitter won't be scouring your shelves and chowing down on your six-dollar organic potato chips and fancy sparkling water.

- *Have good television channels or an excellent DVD collection.* Your basic cable and Baby Einstein DVDs are not going to cut it. If you're not a television watcher, then make sure you've got a plethora of great movies for the sitter to watch or wireless so she can surf the Internet while you're out painting the town. And make sure the sitter knows how to use the remote. You don't want to be interrupted with a frantic call because she can't figure out how to turn up the volume on your stereo system.

- ***Be generous.*** Find out what the average hourly rate is for babysitters in your area and pay the sitter a dollar more. For popular sitters, that extra dollar could be the difference between getting you first priority on their list of families or being dropped way down at the bottom.

If you're worried about the sitter handling your extremely intricate bedtime routine, then just put your kid down before you head out and grab drinks and dessert instead. If the late-night date doesn't fit well with your schedule, then try a breakfast or lunch rendezvous. It might take a few tries before you figure out what works best for you as well as for your kids, but once you do, make it a regular, scheduled occurrence in your weekly or monthly calendar. And if you're concerned about leaving your kids with a babysitter, realize that now your chatty little toddler or preschooler will give you a full report the next day.

MOMINATRIX SAYS

You're not doing yourselves or your kids any favors by letting them take over your entire house. It's okay to have a mom and dad room, mom and dad furniture, and mom and dad stuff. They'll make more empathic human beings when they leave the house knowing that the sun does not rise and set because of them.

Playing Together Means Staying Together

Another way you can reconnect with your partner is by taking up some sort of communal hobby. And no, mutual masturbation does not count as a "hobby."

Finding common interests outside of your kids is one of the smartest things you can do, especially since your kids won't always be the center of your lives. It might be hard to imagine right now, when you're knee deep in T-ball, ballet class, and all sorts of teeny-tiny toys that somehow end up in your toilet, but it won't always be that way. And really, it shouldn't even completely be that way now.

So pick an activity that you have both wanted to do but just never had the chance because you had a baby, or one that you both engaged in before you had kids but just haven't gotten around to starting back up again. If you're feeling brave or generous, try taking up something that your partner really enjoys but you've previously refused to consider. That doesn't mean your husband should join you in your scrapbooking obsession or that you need to dive head-first into the world of fantasy football, but it's definitely worth making a point to enjoy your time together doing something other than staring at a television next to each other or shoving food down your throat.

Whether it's joining a gym together, taking up golf, or signing up for a cooking class, find something that might interest both of you and go for it. Spending money will probably make you more apt to stick with it, and the regularity of the activity might just be the kick in the ass that your relationship needs. Plus, when you retire, you won't be sitting around waiting for your kids to call.

Going Away

The idea of leaving your kids for a few days—hell-even just overnight—can send some parents into a full-blown anxiety attack. But going away together can be a fantastic reward for surviving the baby months or years, and it can really do wonders for your relationship. Plus it allows you to fully reap the benefit of grandparents.

MOMINATRIX SAYS

If you really want to add a little romance into the mix, take ballroom dancing lessons. It might be tough to get your partner on board, but going with a few other couples can make it much more fun. Plus, if you make it apparent that it's a clear way to get in your pants, you can bet he'll have his dancing shoes on in no time.

Of course, a few planets have to be perfectly aligned in order for this to all come to fruition, but it's clearly not as complicated or scary as it sounds. For one thing, before you think that going away means a weeklong cruise or a couple of weeks on a beach in Hawaii, then you might want to adjust your expectations. Sure, a full seven days away from the munchkins does sound pretty orgasmic. And if you can hack being away from your kids that long, or really, trust your family members with your kids that long, then by all means, go for it.

But if time and budget are an issue, you should know that going away together doesn't mean you have to go on a cross-country vacation. You can have just as much fun spending a night in a downtown hotel or at a quaint, local bed and breakfast. Depending on where you live, you've probably got a host of options, maybe even discounted ones, for parents like you who are trying to spend a peaceful, romantic night away from their kids.

Don't be surprised if you feel incredibly apprehensive about leaving your kids, or decide that maybe a family vacation isn't such a bad idea after all. But just take a moment to imagine a quiet, romantic dinner, followed by a bubble bath and a night of uninterrupted lovemaking, and you'll probably change your mind pretty quickly. And really, your kids could probably use a little break from you just as much as you could use a little break from them. Just remember: Regardless of how much credit you want to take for raising your kids, it's not rocket science. They'll be fine. And so will you.

MOMINATRIX SAYS

Remember that your parents or your in-laws raised you and your partner and kept you alive and kicking for many years, so worry more about what you're going to do with all your free no-kids time and less about how your kids will survive without you.

GETTING CAUGHT

Now your journey to relight your fires within shouldn't completely exclude playing with matches in the bedroom. You are humans and not robots, so by all means, have at it. You know, after you've caught up on sleep, that is.

However, the startlingly quick transition from babyhood to toddlerdom can take even the most prepared parent off guard. One minute they're chewing on a dog toy with their two tiny teeth and the next minute they're walking in on you while you're doing the deed.

Here's hoping you've been putting aside money for long-term therapy or intensive psychiatric care along with that 529 College Savings Plan.

Truth be told, most kids aren't hugely traumatized by seeing their parents having sex, but when asked, they can almost always offer a scarily detailed recount of the exact moment in time when it happened. It's like a childhood rite of passage: first broken bone, first kiss, first time you saw your naked parents going at it.

On the bright side, it's not such a bad thing for your kids to see that you actually still care about each other enough to send the very best pelvic thrusts that your old haggard body can muster. In fact, it should really give them hope that after pushing out a few little rugrats you're not institutionalized. After all, sex is a normal human act. Too bad you're dealing with kids who already think you're a couple of weirdos from another planet.

How to Handle It

Now before you go off and feel guilty for something that has yet to actually occur, keep in mind that the amount of memory and possible trauma depends on how old your kids are, and exactly what you were doing when they caught you. For instance, you were probably able to distract your babies and wee toddlers from your butts in the air pretty easily with some type of television program or candy-related bribe. No damage done—and better, no explanation or lengthy discussion required. You can even get back to the merry deed.

But with preschoolers, electronic devices can only keep them occupied for so long. Ten minutes into the movie and they need a snack or their butt swiped and suddenly they're standing there with a box of Cheddar Bunnies and a roll of toilet paper staring straight at your naked boobs bouncing in the breeze.

So if they do happen to bust in on you during the act, it's probably best to address the situation in simple terms as opposed to just letting it go—or worse, making a big deal out of it. The last thing you want is for your kid to bring it up at school the next day during show and tell. Or in this case, just tell.

THE MOMINATRIX'S GUIDE TO EXPLAINING SEX TO YOUR PRESCHOOLER	
Missionary position	Wrestling
Side by side	Hugging
Woman on top	Horsey rides
Sex in the shower	Deep cleaning (or saving water, for you tree huggers)
Oral sex	Um, good luck on that one

As far as the older kids are concerned, clearly you don't want your ass being the big topic of discussion at the next sleepover party. Because while you'd like to think your kids have more to talk about than So-and-So's mom and dad bumping Wookies on a Saturday night, just remember what you talked about as a kid at those sort of gatherings. You'll quickly realize that they'll probably be shoving their mouths full of Twizzlers and popcorn as your kid gives them the play-by-play.

This is not to say that you shouldn't be free to experience your lovemaking any which way and in any place you choose. But considering you've all heard those stories—complete with sound effects—of how parents used to close the door every Saturday afternoon and "have mommy and daddy time," if you think kids don't have a clue, think again. They probably know exactly what you're doing and are listening to you through the door with a strategically placed glass. Except now kids have cell phones with voice recorders and cameras. Best not underestimate the power of your technologically savvy child.

So when it comes to having sex while kids are old enough to spill the beans to every Tom, Dick, and Mother-in-Law inhabiting your house, you might want to create a plan of attack before banging without discretion.

The Mominatrix's Guide to "Safe" Sex

1. *Set boundaries.* If your kids are old enough to play in their rooms alone with the doors closed, then they're old enough to respect your closed doors as well. Take the time to discuss what it means when your doors are shut, and how they should get your attention if they need you when the doors are closed. Knocking politely? Yes. Screaming *fire*? No. Start the road to mutual respect early and it will pay big dividends later.

2. *Lock the door.* While locking the door might seem like a logical predecessor to sex as a parent, before you had little ones, you probably never really had a reason to use your door locks. But now that you

might actually want a little privacy, definitely make sure to use them before doing the deed. Then you won't have to conjure up some ridiculous story. And if you don't have a lock on your door, buy those baby-proofing door handle protectors. While it might not keep your little smarty-pants out of your room, it'll give you a bit of warning before Junior storms in.

3. *Use the covers.* If you're really worried that your kids will walk in, then make sure anything you do is kept under wraps. Literally. While it might limit a few of your crazy positions, you won't be permanently damaging your children with the sight of your naked ass in the air.

4. *Keep sex in the bedroom.* You may have to resort back to the boring bedroom until your kids can be trusted to survive on their own for a few minutes or hours. Being caught in your bedroom will give you an easy segue into a conversation about privacy. Doing it on the kitchen counter is a little more difficult to explain to a poor unsuspecting kid looking for a snack.

5. *Do it when your kids aren't home.* If you really want to play it safe, just don't have sex when the kids are home. But be sure that you know their schedule and keep track of time. Just because they're off with Grandmom or at a friend's house doesn't mean you've got all day to lay around naked. The only thing worse than seeing the look on your kids' face when they catch you having sex is having them watch as you desperately scramble for clothes.

Now if your kids do happen to catch you in the middle of lovemaking, the last thing you want to do is freak out. Seeing you going at it was probably punishment enough, so don't add insult to injury and paint sex as a carnal sin. Connecting sex with guilt or shame, especially from an early age, can cause a whole host of problems later on, as many of you probably already know.

Depending on how old they are, calmly tell them to go to their room. Then once you've gotten all your parts back in your pants, bathed yourself in holy water, and had a chance to laugh about it, take the time to talk with them about what actually went down—in age-appropriate language, of course.

The Mominatrix's Helpful Hints to Talking to Your Kids about Sex

1. *Don't ignore the signs.* Whether you're superstitious, religious, or completely oblivious, if your kids walk in on you, this is the perfect opportunity to start the sex dialogue. And whatever your reasons have been for putting it off, take the bull by its horns and go for it. You'll be glad you did when they start coming home from school with all sorts of questions about things you didn't think they were old enough to know about.

2. *Prepare what you're going to say.* Don't just decide on the fly that tonight's the night to talk about sex. In this case, spontaneity is probably not your friend. While you can't plan when the opportunity

will present itself, you can be ready for when it does.

3. *Keep it simple and serious.* You're talking to kids, so you probably don't want to get into a college-level discussion on human anatomy. Still, that doesn't mean you should dumb-down body part names into baby talk. Leave the "pee-pees" and the "woo-woos" out of the equation and just give them clear information based on what you think they can handle.

4. *Let them ask questions.* After you address the issues at hand, encourage your kids to ask any questions that they might have. In the long run, you want them to get information from you, not their goofy school friends—or worse, the Internet.

5. *It's uncomfortable, but get over it.* If you'd rather have teeth pulled than talk to your kids about sex, you're not alone. But think about all the crazy, misguided assumptions that you had about sex courtesy of your prude parents, and perhaps you'll be a bit more inclined to take the time to sit down and do the deed—er, have "the talk." Plus, if you're squirming and sweating, then you'll be sending the wrong message to your kids. So if you can't get over your fear, fake it.

Regardless of what you've decided to discuss with your children, make a point to emphasize the issue of privacy in general, which is an important thing for every kid to learn, no matter how old they are. This way, you can be certain that you'll never be traumatized by walking in on *their* private time.

As your kids get older, life doesn't necessarily get easier—it just gets different. So don't sit around waiting for that so-called perfect time to enjoy your relationship with your partner. Take advantage of your kids' newfound independence before it's too late and your flame takes more than a match to ignite.

9

SPICING
IT UP

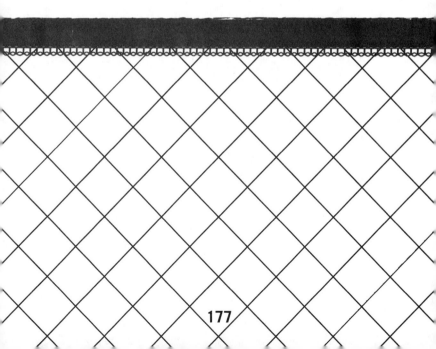

Effectively hopping back on the sex wagon is only the first battle when it comes to managing sex within a parenting relationship. Undoubtedly, if you haven't had sex for a while, or if you are on a sex schedule like Aunt Flo—basically, once a month—then keeping things hot and exciting might not be an issue. In fact, actually having sex might be such a shock to your system that it's enough to make and keep you horny.

But quite frankly, no one eats the same thing for dinner every night. And for good reason.

Even eating the same meal once a week, on the same plate and at the same temperature, can get old pretty fast. So the same old sex? *Snore.*

That's not to say you can't survive on the same sex over and over again, but when tweaking a few aspects of your sex life can change the excitement level from manageable to totally out of control, why not give it a try? And besides, there's a huge difference between surviving and enjoying yourself. You *could* eat bread every day and drink only water, but when you could savor an amazing meal every night of the week, or even just one out of seven, then it's definitely worth it.

For some parents, the idea of spicing it up means doing it with the lights on. For others it means taking the lovemaking out of the bed and into the closet or car. Whatever your starting point might be, it's best to enjoy the changes in baby steps. For you, maybe watching porn means staying awake for an entire R-rated movie that happens to have a few hot sex scenes. And maybe role playing involves pretending to be a sexy, adult woman in lingerie instead of an old fuddy-duddy in a pair of flannel pajamas.

Changing your bedroom routine is all about having an open mind, setting realistic expectations, and perhaps most of all, not taking yourselves too seriously. Remember what that was like?

HITTING IT OUTSIDE THE SACK

You don't necessarily need to invest large amounts of money on leather whips and rubber suits when it comes to adding a little spice to your love life. Sometimes, it's the incredibly simple things, like having sex at a different time of day, or in this case, in somewhere other than your own bed, that can add a bit of added flavor to your bland lovemaking.

MOMINATRIX SAYS

Actually, if you're looking to enjoy a little public sex, a dressing room in an otherwise abandoned department store is the way to go. You've got a locked door, a secluded area, and if you choose wisely, a handy bench. Just make sure to lay something down on it before you get started.

Think about it. As young, single twenty-somethings, the bed was the last place you probably thought about using for sexual purposes. Sure, it cradled your body after a few drunken escapades, but as far as the horizontal mambo, you equated the bed with old married people with kids.

Perhaps it was a desire to avoid the dreaded roommate walk-in, even with your secret code word scrawled on the hanging white board, or that your boyfriend's bed sheets could have gotten up and opened the door for you. But either way, sex lying down on a bed was the death of any relationship. So while every psychologist in the country is trying to figure out why marriages are collapsing at Mach speed, maybe couples should start the road to recovery by having sex somewhere else other than in their beds.

This is not to say that hopping over to your local JCPenney to find an abandoned menswear dressing room for a quick fuck is going to save a marriage. But it can certainly bring back a level of attention and excitement that you and JCPenney probably haven't seen in a really long time.

Now, having kids can kill any type of adventurous around-the-house sex. Unless you're a design genius, toys are everywhere, and if you're not careful, your daring romp could get you a Lego in the ass. Clearly there are way better choices than a square building toy for that sort of thing. And the thought of screwing on the juice-stained couch that your kids watch television on might also be a hard sell. While it might be a great cover for your grape-flavored lubricant, the thought of your kid's head lying on a spot where your naked butts were slapping together in the heat of passion is a sure fire erection killer.

But don't let a couple of mini-obstacles keep you tied to your bedroom. Here are a few reasons that might just convince you to take the leap out of your bed and into uncharted waters.

When you're the mom of a small baby, you're probably running on fumes. This means that when your head hits the pillow, you do not want to be disturbed. Therefore, you are much more likely to enjoy sex, or at least stay awake during it, if you attempt it somewhere else.

Also, if you haven't noticed having a baby makes you almost freakishly sensitive to sound. If a squeaky bed made you uncomfortable before, then the chance of it—or even just slightly heavier breathing—waking up the baby will probably seal your legs together. With bassinets and cribs in close proximity to your own bed or bedroom, you'll end up being too concerned with waking up the baby to even have a shot of getting it on. And if you're co-sleeping, then you've got a baby in your bed. And no matter how comfortable you think you are, the last thing you want to see while you're banging, other than your mother-in-law, is your kid's face.

And finally, babies force you into a pretty predictable existence. A regular schedule of diaper changes and feedings take up most of what can often be a fairly boring day. With that in mind, capitalize on this change to break free from the chains of babydom and leave the bed for its original purpose.

Moving your lovemaking out of the bed doesn't require much planning or thought—an always helpful benefit when you barely have the energy to actually do the deed, let alone prepare another location. Just take a look around your house and figure out what might be a titillating place to get it on. And if you're feeling especially motivated, you can even use it as an incentive to clean your house. If there's anything that will inspire you to vacuum, the prospect of rolling your body around in the remains of an afternoon snack might just do the trick.

PORN FOR PARENTS

Before that evil four-letter word sends you running for the hills with your rosary firmly grasped in your sweaty palm, you should probably know that porn has certainly made great strides and strokes over the last few years. There are actually pornographic movies with story lines, good-looking men, and none of that weird music that they play on exercise DVDs. But, for the most part, the majority of pornography is probably not anything you'd want to be caught dead watching—or worse, catch your partner staring blankly at with his hand down his pants. There's a good chance that instead of feeling turned on, you'll find yourself staring like a rubber-necker on the highway and not enjoying it in a way that makes it worth your while. The idea is to bring the spark back into your love life, not freak you out to the point that the thought of sex makes you feel very, very dirty.

Satisfying Different Tastes

Introducing porn into a relationship can be a risky venture, mainly because what appeals to a guy might not necessarily appeal to a gal. The last thing you need is to tell your significant other that you're interested in watching some porn together and have him pop in some ridiculous DVD of a fairly attractive woman giving out blowjobs while getting screwed in the ass. That doesn't lend itself well to the mystery, seduction, or intrigue that tends to turn women on. You want porn to be exciting for both you and your partner, and not a reason to enter marriage counseling and comb through your credit card bill for sex website membership fees.

And when you think about it, dads aren't the ones needing a libido boost. After all, the bleary-eyed nursing mother isn't usually the one racking up two-hundred-dollar-a-night bills from live-sex chat rooms at 2 A.M., although a few orgasms courtesy of "bigdick79" might make those wee-hour-of-the-morning feedings worth her while. So why sit through some dude boning a hot, big-boobed, lipo-bellied woman, or two lusciously gorgeous women going at it? That's probably not going to do much for the tired postpartum mom except make her want to vomit.

Of course, all porn is not aimed at the male species, and with some quick searches, you'll be able to find a plethora of female-friendly movies. For the most part, the female porn market is growing by leaps and bounds. Apparently they finally figured out that women might enjoy watching porn if it didn't involve a bunch of women being sexually degraded by some big, ugly, naked dude. And for many women, the only way to guarantee foreplay is to watch it happen on the screen, not to rely on their actual partner to provide it for them.

MOMINATRIX SAYS

If you're in the market for lady-friendly porn, take a look at the work of Candida Royalle from Femme Productions *(www .candidaroyalle.com)*. Her DVDs are classic favorites that emphasize female pleasure.

Even so, lady porn is still porn, and as parents, stopping over at your local adult video store on the way back from grocery shopping with your kids strapped in the back of the station wagon probably isn't the smartest thing you've ever done. And while the Internet has opened the proverbial porn floodgates, with websites offering parent-friendly picks and discrete ordering, keeping your slew of DVDs out of the grubby little hands of nosy little babies and toddlers can be quite the challenge. With your luck, you'd pop *Dora the Bi-curious Explorer* into the wrong case and that special "birds and bees" speech you had reserved for a later date would need to be delivered impromptu.

Now don't feel like some closet freak if watching two, three, or twenty-nine people go at it is the quick fix that you and your partner need to get the love juices flowing again. No one—not even the trusty customer service agent who will ensure that your *Debbie Does Dallas* DVD arrives undamaged—will judge you. But when given the choice, most women could care less about the lighting, breast size, and actual penetration; they prefer a movie with a believable story line.

The Best Cable Has to Offer

So instead of forking over way too much money on extremely predictable movies like *Forrest Hump*, which you'll probably just fast-forward through anyway, why not try a few cable or Netflix options that can put you in the mood almost instantly—no brown-paper wrapper or special lockbox required. Not only will this eliminate the feeling that you need to take three showers after viewing, but you won't have to worry about your "Mommy and Daddy Movies" getting into the wrong little hands.

Sex and the City Reruns

So while you might have to pay your partner in blow-jobs to get him to watch it with you, specific episodes, like the ones in which Carrie and Big have their affair or Samantha bangs the fireman, could have you and him putting out in no time. Plus there's at least one very satisfied naked person in every episode, which isn't bad for a regular old cable television show.

HBO's Trifecta of Sex Shows: Real Sex, Pornucopia, The Cat House

Although these shows often feature the quirky and truly bizarre, they are parent porn in the guise of a "documentary"—perfect for educational types or parents who want something a little racier than a plain old television show. Unfortunately, there seems to be absolutely no rhyme or reason when it comes to the schedule of these shows, so make sure to enlist the assistance of your trusty DVR or TiVo. And this way, you can watch a few episodes in a row if you're in need of a little extra help.

True Blood

So clearly vampires are an acquired taste, but if you're a fan of racy supernatural drama, then you'll want to make sure to catch this show. Based on the popular Sookie Stackhouse book series, *True Blood* tells the tale of a telepathic barmaid who hangs with vampires. Don't worry. Thanks to synthetic blood, there's not a ton of neck biting going on. Or at least the kind that kills humans, anyway. And since this show is obviously fantastical in nature, the plots are more like actual porn.

Mad Men

Set in the 1960s, this hit AMC show focuses on the professional and personal life of ad executive Don Draper. The combination of intrigue, soap opera–style story lines, and award-winning performances will keep you and your partner coming back for more. And the men aren't just mad. They're hot.

Californication

Showtime has turned up the heat with *Californication,* a show starring David Duchovny as a novelist who's got a penchant for sex, so much so that you might accidentally mistake it for soft-core porn on a quick channel flip. Though the story itself has been criticized as a little cliché, it's worth it just to see Duchovny's ass.

MOMINATRIX SAYS

Don't feel relegated to the watered-down stuff if you'd rather watch the hard-pounding porn. *Velvet Thrust* is an awesome starter porn flick with high production values and realistic story lines that focus on the guys rather than the girls. This makes it perfect for couples.

Raunchy Rentals

While various sources have ranked their top fifty movie sex scenes, your favorites will depend on your own personal preference for what constitutes hot sex. Whether that includes gay or lesbian sex, threesomes, or just plain old, raw "doing it," make sure the movies you pick contain the type of sex you actually find titillating. And since most R-rated movies feature some sort of sex scene, you might want to find a movie that you'd actually consider watching for longer than the scene itself.

MOMINATRIX SAYS

Not sure if a toy is right for you? Don't sweat it. Most reputable online sex shops now have customer reviews, sort of like Amazon. Check the rating and see what the real people have to say before you slap down money for it.

And before you start adding a bunch of these movies into your Netflix queue, make sure the people having sex are hot. Part of the appeal of porn—and a good sex scene, for that matter—is that the people involved are super gorgeous. Sure, Dom DeLuise might have done a sex scene, but that doesn't necessarily mean you ever want to see it.

The Mominatrix's Top Five Movie Sex Scenes

1. *Top Gun.* Maybe it's the sexual tension throughout the movie, or that a young, pre–Looney Tunes Tom Cruise is sort of smokin'. But the scene in Kelly McGillis's bedroom is pretty damn hot. Of course, so is an entire movie full of sexy pilots in uniform.

2. *Atonement.* Though only a brief light in a fairly dark movie, the library love scene between Kiera Knightly and James McAvoy is definitely worth

checking out. Just make sure to turn it off after that scene if you want to get laid.

3. *Original Sin.* No list would be complete without an Angelina Jolie film, and the long, intense sex scene with Antonio Banderas does not disappoint. In fact, it might just even make you blush, mostly courtesy of the various shots of Angelina's particularly perfect breasts.

4. *Unfaithful.* While the idea of a mom cheating on her husband with a hot bookseller might not be the most romantic of plots to spice up your marriage, the frequent sexual encounters between Diane Lane and Olivier Martinez will make you feel bad for Richard Gere for about two seconds. And if you happen to be a Richard Gere fan, then you're getting a two-fer.

5. *Out of Sight.* There's just something magical about two gorgeous people doing it, and that's why you'll both enjoy watching Jennifer Lopez and George Clooney get it on in a dark hotel room. Plus you won't feel bad drooling over George when you look over to see your husband's eyes fixated on J.Lo's ass. All's fair.

TOYS, ALL THOSE TOYS

Whether you're an avid sex toy user or haven't pulled out your Rabbit since before you had kids, sex toys can definitely make a mundane sex life much more interesting and satisfying. But other than at the whitewashed, no-window buildings in *that* part of town or those slightly awkward sex toy parties, where does a mom commandeer a handy dandy vibrator these days?

Well, hooray for that little thing called the Internet, which offers you and millions of other horny people discrete access to what would have otherwise required embarrassing visits to the local sex shop. Online stores, particularly those aimed at women, are a far cry from the dirty hole-in-the-walls you've driven by with a mix of curiosity and disgust. On the contrary, they're well organized and chock full of everything you'd find in the shop—just without the skeeviness attached to it. You might even find a butt plug sort of cute. The descriptions, personal recommendations, and helpful instructions take the hassle out of ordering, and they allow you to explore various toys in the privacy of your own home without having to worry about your child asking you what the pretty beads and leather thong underpants are for.

Parent-Friendly Sex Toys

At first glance, you might think the term "parent-friendly" in reference to sex toys is a misnomer, because even though you have kids, you didn't fall off the face of the earth. (Well, yet.) Until you're snuggling up in your own twin bed decked out in footie pajamas with a glass of warm milk, you're still a human with needs, kids or not. So why won't just any old sex toy work for you? Because no mom or dad wants to have a gigantic, eight-inch, battery-operated, bright pink penis lying around their bedroom. Even though your baby won't be able to open your nightstand drawer, that sweet baby will soon be a grabby, nosy toddler. So why not choose a toy that won't force you to attempt to explain to a two-year-old why there's a vibrating wee-wee in your nightstand?

Thanks to the amazing advancements in technology, combined with that little thing you proudly call a clitoris, you don't need a sex toy that actually looks like a real penis. You can find a plethora of toys that are highly effective in getting you off without being blatantly obvious—and that won't make your husband get a little worried that his dick now has some stiff competition. Literally.

These parent-friendly toys (also known as "discrete toys" to you regular sex toy shoppers) eliminate the need for a lock on your special drawer, which is a blessing in disguise if you can't remember your own phone number let alone a lock combination or the location of a teeny set of drawer keys. And if your kiddo does happen to get his hands on them, you won't need to have a birds, bees, and sex toys speech prepared. In fact, a vibrating toy of any kind can keep even the most distracted kid occupied long enough for a diaper change. And knowing some of the things you've let your kid play with just to keep Junior still and occupied for a solid minute, a sex toy probably isn't that ridiculous. Better that than something that looks like your husband's dick.

Just make sure you invest in a little thing called "sex toy cleaner."

The Mominatrix's Top Five Incognito Sex Toys

1. *The Cone.* While it's a bit big to fit into a night-stand drawer, luckily the Cone vibrator can pass as a piece of modern art, displayed proudly on your dresser or vanity. But with sixteen speeds and a hands-free design, the cone might just be a better investment than a weirdly shaped sculpture.

2. *The Lipstick Vibe.* No one will think twice if they catch a glimpse of a lipstick tube on your dresser. You'll want to keep track of this vibrating toy since little girls might decide to add it to their dress-up bin or play purse.

3. *The Flashlight.* This sex toy is actually handy; not only does it vibrate you into ecstasy but it'll ensure that you're not left in the dark during blackouts since your family will be able to see and hear you. Kudos to you for putting safety first.

4. *The Tingletip.* Don't toss your old electric tooth-brushes out. Take an eco-friendly approach and turn them into a vibrator with this small plastic attachment that covers the brush portion. It certainly gives the phrase "brush after every meal" a whole new meaning.

5. *Vortex Vibrations.* You'll never look at your vacuum cleaner the same way once you've met this toy that hooks onto the hose. Granted, the loud drone of your vacuum as you wrestle with your attachment hose might hinder your climax, but at least the neighbors will think you're one fantastic

housekeeper. Too bad you can't use it *while* you vacuum. Now that would be genius.

His and Hers Toys

If you're not so keen on using the single sex toys on each other, or the idea of playing with them on yourself in front of your partner gives you stage fright, then you'll want to take a peek at the slew of toys that are meant to be enjoyed together during intercourse. It can be a bit awkward trying to get your partner to try out something that he actually might have to wear, but with a little coercion, you'll have no problem getting him to join in on the fun.

Vibrating Cock Rings

Before you hide your head in the sand, you have to give this extremely popular couple's toy a try. Available in almost every variety, including leather and rubber (depending on your preference and pubic hair situation), it provides clitoral stimulation during intercourse and keeps him going and going and going. For a cock ring that doesn't look like a freak show reject, the Bo is a discrete option (in shape and name) that's still highly effective.

MOMINATRIX SAYS

When it comes to cock rings, skip the rubber and go with leather. While they might look a bit hardcore, they're way easier on the pubic hair.

The We-Vibe

If you're not sure you can convince your partner to try on a toy of his own, then you can be the very happy guinea pig with the We-Vibe. It has two vibrating pods, and *you* wear it during intercourse. This toy stimulates your G-spot as well as your clitoris, both at the same time. While it might seem like a lot to "take in," keep in mind that you birthed a baby out of that hole, so you should have no issues with a bit of extra girth. Plus, your partner might get a little enjoyment from the vibration as well.

Remote-Control Vibes

For a little fun outside of the bedroom, you might want to invest in a remote-control vibe. Pop the vibrating piece into your underpants and hand the remote over to your partner. He can get you started throughout dinner, or while you're both working around the house. If you're feeling extra daring, get your cell phone involved with the Boditalk Escort. Hook up the special attachment so that when he calls, your phone vibrates on your special place.

ROLE PLAYING

Unless you met your partner at a Trekkie convention, chances are that trying to get you to dress up as something other than a tired, overworked mother might be pretty tough. That doesn't mean role playing and fantasy in the bedroom can't work. Anything that takes away the reminder that in a few hours you'll be dragging your sleepy body into your kid's room for Junior to suck on your boob for a solid ten minutes would be a welcome addition to your sex life. And wearing something other than a nursing bra and loosely fitting underpants might be just the fix any mom could use to make sex a little more interesting. But chances are, if your husband told you he wanted you to dress up like Lois Lane to his Superman, you'd laugh him right out of the house.

When it comes to dressing up and fantasy role playing (if you're being official with terminology), you can't just go from barely naked parent sex to a Princess Leia and Han Solo seduction scene without at least one of you dying from a combination of embarrassment and laughter. Many parents have a hard time pitching their partner a different sexual position, let alone some elaborate role-playing situation that involves an actual script. And while egos and self-esteem should be firmly in place, hearing your partner say that he'd like you to dress up like someone else might not be the best way to get the hot and heavy back in your love life. It's one thing if he wants you to wear a rabbit costume, but if he's asking you to put on a blonde wig and big fake boobs while he calls you Pam, you might not be so inclined to participate in the charade. Similarly, expecting your easygoing partner to suddenly throw on a loin cloth and ravage you like Tarzan might be taking things a bit too far.

The benefits of fantasy play in a sexual relationship certainly outweigh the risks—excluding those rare fetishes that include husbands who dress up in lacy thongs or both parties who wear furry animal suits. But generally speaking, adding an element of fantasy can be just what parents need to get out of their sexual rut.

Undergarments

While a brand-new, shiny pair of underpants or some hot lingerie might not be considered a costume to some people, for many moms out there, just wearing a thong might make their partner wonder who the hell they are. So instead of going to bed in your typical parental pajamas, try wearing something your "former" self might have worn. Even a very simple and inexpensive change such as a skimpy nightgown for you and a pair of boxer briefs for him could add a little "umph" back into your boring routine. *Feeling risqué?* Try a garter belt and some sexy stockings.

Accessories

You don't necessarily need an entire costume in order to make life a little more interesting. Take a part of your favorite fantasy and see how it works. Try sex with just your boots on or riding your partner sidesaddle with a cowboy hat. It's a great excuse to go shopping for some new accessories, and it can certainly make things way more interesting without requiring you to set foot in a costume shop. And you never know, once you've done it a few times, you might be able to add some chaps and a lasso.

Feeling risqué? Bring back the Vaudeville days with a set of pasties.

Business Attire

Many couples have partners who wear some type of work uniform. Whether it's a brown or white delivery uniform, or a regular old business suit, most parents don't think about incorporating their already existing work attire into the bedroom.

Granted, no one will want to jump you in your dirty scrubs, so make sure you've got something set aside for special circumstances. But consider upping your sex time to some hour *before* bedtime, and welcome your partner home with a special treat while your kids watch *Sponge-Bob Squarepants* on a loop.

Feeling risqué? Strippers have to work too, right? Grab a sexy bikini and some crazy high stilettos.

Playing Dress Up

If a new pair of underwear just isn't going to cut it and you really want to try some actual role playing, then go for more realistic situations rather than something right off the SyFy channel. It's not totally impossible, but it's highly unlikely that some hot cop will stop you for speeding and then decide that in order for you to get out of a ticket, you'll have to give him oral sex. So instead of starting out with a fantasy in full costume, try reenacting the situation using a few props. Maybe your partner is a massage therapist seducing his client or a hot delivery person asking for more than just a signature before leaving. These scenarios aren't so far off the deep end that you'll just end up giggling the entire time. Then, once you think you're both sold on the fantasy, you can always work yourselves up to actual costumes.

Feeling risqué? Hit the costume shop, grab a wig, and go for it.

And always keep in mind that just because your significant other wants you to dress up, it doesn't mean your partner thinks you're not attractive anymore. Sometimes the opportunity to be someone else, if only for a few minutes, can save your sex life and your sanity. So if you're a bit hesitant to take on another persona, think twice. Taking a break from being a mom can be a welcome change.

Well, except if he asks you to wear a mask and keep it on all day long. Then you've got a problem on your hands.

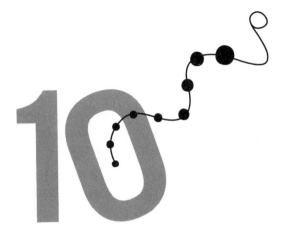

10

THE
UNMENTIONABLES

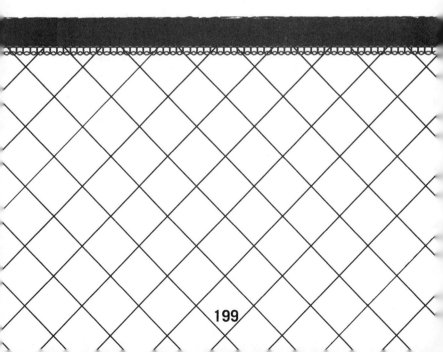

So maybe a switch from having sex in the bed to doing it in the tub was all the spice your sex life needed. But some parents have more demanding taste buds that are not easily satisfied by a puny new sex toy or a splashy pair of underpants.

Whether you've thought about dabbling in more risqué escapades but didn't know where to start, or you're just wondering what happens after you've worn out all the batteries in your Rabbit, then you'll be pleased to know there are plenty more sexual adventures you can explore without feeling like a complete weirdo or a sexual deviant.

That being said, you probably don't want to ask your neighbor where the closest S&M club is in your town. It can be pretty challenging to find resources that offer enlightened information without being explicit. And even worse, once you do find anything on your exotic topic of choice, you don't want to embarrass yourself right out of the idea in the first place.

Most regular bookstores won't offer anything more than *The Joy of Sex,* and a few free hours to peruse your local sex shop probably isn't anywhere in your near future. And while the Internet will certainly open up the Pandora's Box of alternative sexual interests—all of which are just a click away—they're not exactly sites you want to spend any more than two seconds on for fear that they'll contaminate your laptop with some sexually transmitted computer virus. Plus, the last thing you need is for your babysitter to happen upon your search history.

But just because you need to do a bit more digging around to find answers to your burning questions doesn't make you a freak. Many parents have an interest in exotic sexual pleasures but don't necessarily know how to make it happen without scaring their partners. So here are a few extra-naughty extracurricular activities that will take your sex life from tired to titillating with help from some special equipment, a little bit of bravery, and a very open mind.

YOU'RE ON CANDID CAMERA

So you've heard couples joking about making their own movies, and you giggle about it right along with them. But the more you think about it, the more you're intrigued. Don't feel bad. A new celebrity sex tape makes its way to the shelves on a weekly basis, so you're certainly not the only one with the desire to play Martin Scorsese and Jenna Jameson all at once. At least you don't have to worry about the whole world trying to get their paws on live footage of you giving head to your partner.

It makes sense, in a way, that if you're going to watch someone having sex as a means to jumpstart your own engine, it might as well be you and your partner. Better to have your partner lusting after your own postpartum ass than some twenty-year-old porn star who's already pumped full of Botox and silicone.

Now if you're someone who can't stand listening to your own voice on an answering machine, then you might want to think long and hard before recording yourself having sex. If the sound of your voice makes you cringe, just imagine what your nude body will do. Regardless of its current shape and size, if you blow it up on your gigantic television in full Technicolor without the bad music in the background as a distraction, it just might make you faint. And that's probably not the effect you're going for. So unless you're married to Jerry Bruckheimer, then be prepared to see yourself and your partner in all your unedited naked glory.

Setting the Scene

Once you've swallowed that aspect of your new role as a self-made porn star, the actual filming requires a fair amount of planning, which as a parent can be a pretty difficult feat. That doesn't mean that it's not possible, but if you're tending to a frequently waking baby, it's definitely going to affect the mood. Of course, watching you run out of the room half naked to tend to a screaming baby could be entertaining, but perhaps not in the way that you intended it. If you want a good laugh, you can probably find a bunch of other things to watch than your own sex tapes.

Setting up a camera to catch the action doesn't lend itself well to spontaneity, but thanks to technology, it's not that time-consuming to pop your camera up on a dresser. Just make sure you do a few outtakes so you don't end up with the tops of your heads bobbing up and down, or your feet flailing around.

MOMINATRIX SAYS

If you're serious about videotaping, invest in a tripod. You'll still have to check the camera angles but you won't need to put it on top of a pile of books or propped up on your jewelry box.

"I'm Ready for My Close-Up"

Once you've got the camera situation figured out, you should probably be most concerned with how you're going to look on camera. You're not a drunk socialite or Playboy Bunny, but rather, a tired mom who's probably spent a good part of her day running after kids. You might want to be prepared before you memorialize yourself in your birthday suit. And unless you have some fancy night-vision video camera, you're going to have to do it with the lights on.

So if you're going to record yourself completely naked in the bright lights of your bedroom, you'll want to be sure you're feeling and looking your best. Creating a video is exciting in and of itself, but the point is that you'll actually watch it again. And since the camera tends to add fifteen pounds with clothes on, then plan on a good solid twenty for your naked ass.

MOMINATRIX SAYS

If you're not feeling at your best for your appearance, take a cold shower. It actually helps tighten and shrink everything down. Just make sure your partner doesn't join you. You'll need him at his peak performance for your recording session.

Since you won't actually have a cameraperson, you won't need to worry about close-ups, but it might be wise to do a little lady-scaping and personal grooming prior to the big event. Not only will it make you feel sexier, but if your leg or bush happens to flash by the lens, you won't scare yourselves.

However, if you're not feeling your best or just aren't yet comfortable with the idea of being naked on camera, then just wear a few strategically placed items of clothing. In fact, sex with clothes on can be just as hot, if not hotter. You will want to make sure that you actually have something that's camera-ready. If you've got the typical wardrobe of most moms, then you might need to invest in some undergarments that won't make you look like, well, a mom. That doesn't mean you need to spend your grocery money on some fancy corset and garter set that will never see the light of day after your onscreen performance. Better, find items that strategically nip and tuck, and that you'll actually wear again, regardless of whether the camera is on you or not.

Hiding the Evidence

Now if there's anything to prepare for prior to and following your video escapades, it's the labeling and storing of your videos. Unless you feel a divorce is imminent or that your partner might post the videos on the Internet to help pay for a new plasma television, you'll just want to make sure that the videos are clearly marked and kept far, far away from anywhere your kids might find them.

While you might not want to mark them "Mom and Dad Have Sex" or "Missionary Position Take 1," you'll want to name them something that you won't forget, but that won't be so disguised that someone might accidentally pop them into the DVD player. You do not want to become your babysitter's evening entertainment. Of course, any confusion can be avoided by ensuring that you store them in a place that cannot be breached by little people, preferably something with a lock and combination or key.

Once you've worked out all the logistical details, then you'll just want to have fun. Don't decide to re-create some sexual fantasy or act out a scripted scene. Just go about business as usual. And instead of trying to make it your best performance, just let the camera run. You can worry about editing later.

MOMINATRIX SAYS

Don't decide that this is the time for gymnastics sex. Stick with what you know and what you're good at. You don't want to record yourself getting injured.

There's a good chance that you might have a hard time forgetting that the camera is on. For most people, sex is an inherently private act, so it's only natural for you to be a little freaked out by the flashing red light. If you and your partner really want to watch a couple of naked fools having sex, then you might want to just grab something on pay-per-view rather than go through the trouble of making your own.

TIE ME UP

If you already love being ravaged while attached to the bed with a pair of fuzzy handcuffs, then guess what? You've already entered the deep dark world of bondage. You probably thought that since your handcuffs were lined with fur and your husband wasn't calling you

"Mistress," you weren't engaging in what tends to get a really bad rap.

Okay, so the whole thought of getting tied up with chains as you're being whipped on the backside can seem a little scary. But not everything about bondage and S&M (short for *sadomasochism*) has to do with a ball gag and leather masks. At its core, S&M is more about domination and submission, both of which you can definitely relate to if you have children. In fact, a parent's everyday existence is a battle between those very concepts. The only difference there is that you're being dominated by a small little person who's beating you into submission with piercing screams and dirty diapers.

Just because you endure your own form of S&M on a daily basis doesn't mean you should avoid it in the bedroom. You might actually find that playing with the idea of control can be pretty damn sexy. And don't think you need to invest in a latex suit and spiky heels, or remodel your basement into the form of a dungeon. Rather, just play around with who's the boss and see where it leads you.

It's only natural that you'd be turned on by the idea of control. Even if you share the household duties equally with your partner, your kids are probably the ones in control of when you wake up, when you pee, and when you don't get more than a few hours of sleep in a row. Basically, your life is being run by a bunch of little people. So if you need to exercise your big-person status, put yourself back in charge and call the shots in the bedroom.

On the other hand, maybe letting your partner take over could be the welcome break that you need. You don't necessarily need someone to bark orders at you while tugging at a leash around your neck, but relinquishing responsibility and letting go while someone else takes care of business, without your input for once, could be pretty damn hot.

Whichever role you decide to take, it's important to start slowly and gently. So purchase a set of handcuffs and then let your imagination run wild.

The Mominatrix's Top Five Fun Things to Enjoy While Handcuffed

1. *Candles.* Who said hot wax was just for hair removal? Grab a couple of special candles, light them up, and drip the melted wax on a few strategic areas, particularly the super-sensitive nipples. Don't worry. It only burns for a few seconds.

2. *Feather dusters.* While dusters aren't the most effective way to clean your house, they can certainly do a number on your inner thighs. Brush lightly over your partner's skin and watch your significant other wriggle in delight. Just avoid the feet if you've got a super-ticklish partner.

3. *Blindfolds.* Take away the ability to see and you're forced to rely on all your other senses, thus heightening your overall sexual experience. Make sure to stimulate with sounds, touch, and even smell. Good ones, that is.

4. *Chocolate syrup and other edibles.* Playing around with food in the bedroom can be satisfying for both parties. While any old items you have in the fridge will work, you might try ones that are made specifically for skin application. A case of hives is never really that sexy. And depending on how well your kids sleep, you can extend your exciting evening with a shower in case you weren't able to get all that syrup off with your tongue.

5. *Body paints.* Let your inner Leonardo da Vinci out and go to town on your partner. The combination of the cool paint along with the soft swirl of the brush is sure to satisfy. For extra fun, track down edible body paints. Just make sure you put down a towel or keep an extra set of sheets close by.

Now, if you're a bit more intrigued by the world of whips and nipple clamps, then you might have to do a bit more coaxing. However, you did decide to have kids, so you've probably had your nipples clamped and your butt whipped at one point in time or another. So doing it for sexual pleasure shouldn't be such a far cry.

DOIN' THE BUTT

Contrary to popular belief, it's not just porn stars, ass men, and that ambiguously gay college boyfriend of yours who just so happened to own every single Cher album who like the butt play. Regular old moms dig the butt action too.

Granted, the post-baby butt can be a bit more complicated to stimulate, particularly when even you need a map to insert your own hemorrhoid suppositories and the thought of your poor bedraggled asshole makes you fear your daily bowel movement.

Don't gag. If you've had a baby, you can relate.

But when all the other obvious spots on your postpartum body have otherwise been dulled by the joys of childbirth and baby feeding, the butt can be an extremely sensitive and arousing area. That is, if you can get around the whole poop thing. It is a butthole, after all.

If you deal with poop on a regular basis, like most moms do or have done at one time or another, in theory it shouldn't be a big deal. You stare at tiny butts and wipe them more than you'd prefer, so messing around with a bigger one should be familiar territory.

But truthfully, there aren't many people who actually enjoy the smell of fresh shit on their finger, or better, wafting in the air mixed with sweat during a massive lovemaking feast. In most cases, that instantly kills the mood. Hell, most husbands can barely change a diaper without gagging. No matter how much they're excited about taking their boat down the chocolate river, the smell of poop will most definitely change their mind. And considering how much you've got to deal with rear ends every day, they can't expect you to excitedly stick your finger in their butt.

And along with having to deal with the shit scent, there's always the prospect of accidental pooping. If this elicits total mortification for laboring women, then they'll probably feel the same way if it happens in the bedroom.

With all that said, if you're ready to put the perhaps literal "dirty" back into your sex life, then there are a few obvious things that should probably be reiterated.

A Clean Butt Is a Happy Butt

First and foremost, the butt is not the cleanest spot on your body. Surprised? Yeah, probably not. So, if you want someone to play with your backside, or you're offering it up as a new tunnel of love, you should consider cleaning it. Change that; you should absolutely, 100 percent make sure that you could eat off it. In fact, if you do your job well, you might just get that too.

MOMINATRIX SAYS

Most lubes are made with glycerin, which can be mildly irritating for some people. Make sure to test it out on your forearm before you dump it over your private parts. Or if you're allergic, grab a glycerin-free lube.

Cleaning your anus can involve everything from just taking a thorough shower to giving yourself an anal douche, which is fancy for *enema* And when you do take the time to clean things out, you'll eliminate the worrisome accidental pooping scenario as well.

MOMINATRIX SAYS

Enemas aren't as bad as they sound. You can pick them up at any drug store, and it will help make you feel more comfortable with the idea of putting something in when everything has been taken out.

Insertion Not Always Necessary

Once you've cleaned your pipe, there are a few things you can enjoy that have absolutely nothing to do with a large penis or penis-shaped apparatus being inserted in your butt (or hey, vice versa). You most certainly do not need to have full-on anal sex to enjoy the pleasure the ass can offer you. Many people enjoy just a fingertip in their ass just prior to and during their orgasm. Others enjoy analingus or other forms of tongue-to-butt pleasure. And some utilize sex toys like anal beads or butt plugs, either during sex or on their own time.

The most important point that should be clear to your partner is that in order for this to be a successful venture for both of you, it's imperative that you are supremely turned on. So enjoy lots of foreplay and take it slowly.

And in the long scheme of things, it can't be any worse than having a speculum inserted while fourteen random people on the labor and delivery unit examine you. And perhaps you'll find out that not only is your partner an ass man, but you're an ass mama.

The Mominatrix's Quick Guide to Anal Sex Toys

If you're worried that you're entering freakdom when it comes to your sexual appetite, these are all fairly typical aspects of healthy sexual lives. Discuss your ideas with your partner, send a clear message (clean ass in the air tends to get the point across), and shop around for toys that seem interesting and safe to both of you. Even the Grand Canyon would squeeze shut at the sight of some of those dildos.

MOMINATRIX **SAYS**

Make sure any and all of your anal sex toys have a flared base. The last thing you want is a trip to the ER to get a toy removed from your ass.

Butt Plugs

Worn during sex or while you're at the grocery store, butt plugs can provide you with heightened sensation, and they can be a good way to orient your ass to having something inside it. They come in various shapes and sizes, all of which are based on your preference, so start small and then go from there.

Anal Beads

These toys can come as an actual string of beads or in dildo-like form, and are pulled out one by one to provide extra stimulation during sex. Like the butt plugs, anal beads are made to fit a variety of tastes and preferences. You might stick with the shorter strings and dildos, and then once you master the insertion, go for the longer options.

G-Spot Stimulators

Often marketed for men but just as effective for women, G-spot or prostate stimulators are basically vibrators for the butt. What's great about these is that when they're not being used for the G-spots, you can use them for clitoral stimulation as well. You'll want to be sure that you keep them super-clean.

Lube Up

Now if you're going for the big guns, keep in mind that butts do not self-lubricate, so you must be extra-prepared. Regardless of whether you are using a condom or not (on your finger, over a sex toy, or on a penis), you must use lube. Must. And while this might seem fairly obvious, you should never switch back and forth from vaginal to anal sex. Never. That just has really bad things written all over it and you've got enough keeping you awake for way too many hours of the night. You don't want to be nodding in agreement with the actors on those sexual disease commercials in your free time. Sex should be a way to release stress, not add more of it to your already complicated life.

The Mominatrix's Three Favorite Lubes

- *Sliquid Sassy Booty Formula.* Completely glycerin-free, this lube stays slick without getting sticky, and is completely taste and odor free.

- *Good Clean Love.* Created by a mom using all natural ingredients, these lubes smell as great as they work.
- *Emerita.* Made for women by women, the Emerita lubes are safe for condoms, sex toys, and real parts too.

GOING THE GAY WAY

It's really not surprising when after years of quick bangs, skid marks, and ball scratching, women decide that what they really need is the comfort of another woman's bosom. And they're not talking about their moms.

Going the gay way is not really a black-and-white issue, as sexuality (like gender) exists on a continuum, so many people who consider themselves to be "straight" can still have feelings and sexual urges for someone of the same gender.

MOMINATRIX SAYS

As cliché as it might sound, for most women, it's hard to separate out the relationship and the sex. When it comes to bi-curious behavior, you'll want to examine everything, not just what's happening in the bedroom, to try to figure out what's going on and how you can translate that into your current situation.

But thanks to our "all or nothing" society, few moms actually admit to having homosexual desires, except for the time when they were drunk on spring break doing body shots off some half-naked girl. No one you know ever did that now, right? But maybe you suddenly have a gay dream, get turned on by the sight of a naked woman, or even fantasize about doing one—all when stone-cold sober with two babies and a husband warming the La-Z-Boy in the living room with his farts.

Clearly these experiences don't taint your sexuality, nor do they make you any less of a straight, married mother of small humans. More realistically, they just make you a sexual human being.

Women have a bit of an advantage when it comes to exploring their interest in other women. Don't think this is the lame argument that absolves you from cheating if it's with someone of the same gender. Chances are that some twenty-six-year-old dude came up with that rationale to get his girlfriend to do a threesome. But it's clear that girl-on-girl action is decidedly more acceptable in a male-driven society. Hearing a straight man admit that seeing two dudes kiss might be sort of hot doesn't happen so often, and it's certainly not because it never crossed his mind. It's just that he probably shoved it down into his subconscious along with everything else that society deems inappropriate. An honest man is the man who admits to having a gay dream.

So if Ms. Pussy is speaking louder to you than good old Mr. Dick, don't run out and get your pink triangle tattoo just yet. It might not be that you've been moonlighting as a straight person and motherhood has finally allowed you to free yourself of the shackles of heterosexuality. In all likelihood, you're simply in need of a change in not only your sex life, but in the daily interactions between you and your partner. Testosterone can be fantastic in the bedroom, but it usually doesn't lend itself well to a mom who's in need of some tender-loving care and a bit of empathy.

So if you've got the reoccurring lesbian sex dreams or are just finding yourself a little more curious about getting it on with a vagina owner, then here are a few suggestions that might help you make sense out of your newfound desire for another woman.

You Are Not Alone

If you've never had any attraction to someone of the same gender, even at the most remote levels or in some random dream that you can barely remember, you're probably in the extreme minority or you haven't seen Jackie Warner. Seriously. Go Google her now.

Most women will admit to having some interest in another woman, even if it's just being turned on by a naked woman's body or two other women doing it. Have you ever taken a peek at an issue of *Playboy* for more than just the articles? Don't freak out. That doesn't mean you're gay or even bisexual. It might just mean that you're redefining the parameters of the word "hot" in your sexual vocabulary and what you're currently getting in your relationship and in the bedroom just isn't cutting it.

Pick up some girl-on-girl porn and watch it with your partner. Chances are you won't hear him complaining, and it might just be enough to satisfy your inner lesbian.

If you're still unsure about making your wishes known, then keep your personal fantasies personal. Create your own encounters of the female kind when you masturbate.

Sometimes that can be enough to fulfill whatever desires you might be having.

And if all else fails, you can always ask your husband to dress up like a woman. Just be prepared for the ramifications. He might actually really like it. And that is a whole other ball of wax.

Going Down

While you might think you're desiring a woman's body, it could just be that you're dying for more oral sex, which surprisingly enough, many men are too squeamish to offer their partners. But if that's the case, then you should cease and desist any mouth play with his mangy penis and call it even.

There are plenty of ways to make oral sex more stomachable for the male species, many of which don't take much effort. And if you talk to your partner and share how you're feeling, he should be willing to give them a try.

The Mominatrix's Guaranteed Ways to Get Oral

1. *Offer the best head in return.* Since most moms aren't sucking off their husbands on a regular basis, the idea of getting a great blowjob in return might just be the incentive he needs.
2. *Make her pretty.* If you've got a mouthful of bush in your pants, then you might even make things precarious for a porn star. Take some time to get groomed—whether it's on your own or by a professional.

3. *Clean her out.* Okay, so this does not mean douche. Those are just plain bad in general. But do take a shower and make sure things smell like roses before you hop into the sack. You probably don't want anything to do with a pair of day-old, sweaty balls, so you can't blame him if he feels the same way about your vagina.

4. *Get creative.* The power of food and edibles can be used to your advantage. While you don't want to stick anything up in there other than a human appendage, you can play around with different tasty spreads—in moderation, of course. You certainly want to entice him into giving you oral, but a post-session yeast infection is not worth the price.

5. *Don't ask, tell him.* There's just something about a woman shoving her pussy in a guy's face, or telling him to "get down there now" that can really turn a guy on. If he was reluctant to head South before, make sure he knows who's boss.

Tender-Loving Care

If that's not the case, it might be that you need a bit more intimacy than two hairy balls dangling over your head can offer. While it might seem stereotypical to say that women use emotion to establish intimacy, it's actually not far from the truth. Perhaps you just need a softer touch, conversation that doesn't involve the kids, and someone to take care of you for once. So before you run off to your local gay bar, talk to your partner about upping the level of affection and intimacy in your relationship.

If the words "date night" make you cringe, then call it something else, because your relationship really could use some rejuvenation beyond the passing hellos and goodnight kisses before bed. Whether it's breakfast out, lunch in, or a few drinks at a bar on a Saturday night, spend time with your partner that has everything to do with each other and nothing to do with the kids. You might find that you were just missing quality time with him — not the arms of a lady lover.

INTO THE WILD
BLUE YONDER

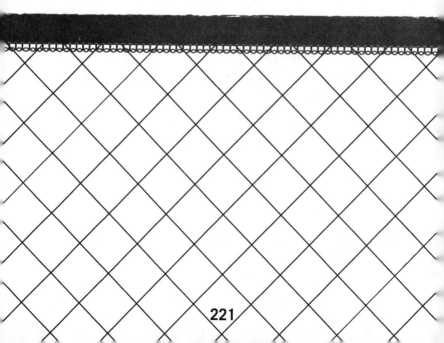

If all this talk about sex hasn't gotten you horny, then at least you should celebrate reading an entire book. That's a pretty stellar accomplishment right there.

But congratulations aside, entering a new sexual phase of your life can be scary, unchartered territory. And although adding kids into the mix doesn't necessarily mean your sex life will automatically lose its fire, for most parents, their sex life after kids can quickly turn into one long road trip full of bumps, potholes, and periods of nothing but terribly boring scenery that they just try to avoid altogether.

Don't let those little munchkins take over your life and knock the wind right out of your sails. Sex only takes a few minutes out of your day; really good sex takes maybe a couple more. And with all the technological advances these days, you can even have sex from a different room or state from your partner. So there's just no excuse. Making time for sex feeds yourself and your relationship, both of which do not function well on empty stomachs.

But wait one second. Before you scamper off with reckless abandon, remember what got you into your position in the first place.

HOW NOT TO GET PREGNANT (AGAIN)

Whether you're just trying to catch your breath before getting knocked up again or you are still deciding if you'll be adding more to your brood, you should probably consider using more than the pullout method for birth control.

And sorry to say that breastfeeding is not effective either. It just gives you a good excuse to keep your husband away from your boobs.

So unless you're up for a surprise in about ten months or you've taken the motherly oath of celibacy, birth prevention should really be a top priority. That also means you might want to avoid particularly fertile times that might get you in a bit of pregnant trouble.

The Mominatrix's Top Three Most Fertile Times of the Year

- *The hours after a holiday party.* If you're wondering why there are so many September and October babies, it's because parents finally get a babysitter, indulge in a bit too much eggnog, and go at it.
- *Reunions after a long absence.* It's true: Absence makes the heart grow fonder. It never fails that when a partner has been gone for a long period of time, the coming-home sex is amazing. And effective.
- *The one night of debauchery and drunkenness.* Having sex on a night when you decide to completely let loose, enjoy way too many tasty beverages, and not remember a single thing the next day is like taking a fertility drug.

Put a Hat On

Now you'd think that after inventing a nuclear bomb, they would have created some type of oral birth control for men that would send the sperm swimming in the wrong direction, or at least render them catatonic for a short period of time. They've figured out how to clone sheep and yet the only way they can prevent sperm from leaving a penis and entering a vagina is by basically putting a cap on it? If that's not a call for women in science, then what is?

Of course, condoms are a fairly effective means of preventing pregnancy, so long as you're diligent enough to actually use them. Unfortunately, keeping a stash in your nightstand doesn't do much for protecting you if you don't open them up and put them on. And while men will continue to whine about how stifling and uncomfortable they are—like someone's put a bag over their head and they're gasping for air—they're usually willing to compromise, particularly if their wives have unfavorable reactions to hormonal birth control.

Count the Days

If condoms aren't an option, some parents decide to use Natural Family Planning, otherwise known as "The Counting Method," which requires the woman to keep track of her cycle (surprise!) and only engage in sex on the least fertile days of the month. This can work famously if you have the willpower of a priest, because for the most part, the days you're going to want to have sex are the ones when you can't have sex. And really, only bionic women tend to have predictable cycles after childbirth.

Besides, with kids in the picture, you've only got a small window of opportunity to get it on. And based on how Murphy's Law usually works with moms and dads, all your kids will be sick and require your round-the-clock care during your monthly sex appointment.

Pills, Shots, and Clips

Of course, the many, many, many options available to women are certainly effective for some and provide adequate prevention when used correctly. The bazillion different kinds of birth control pills can work well, but considering you're probably forgetting the names of your kids these days, good luck trying to remember to take them. And if you're already enjoying a hormonal roller coaster, they might just add more loops and drops to your already scary ride. In fact, you might find your husband willing to buy stock in condoms just to avoid the "Birth Control Bitch."

The same goes for the Depo-Provera shot, which also gives you a 70 percent chance of weight gain and an increased risk of osteoporosis. Just doesn't quite seem to make it worth the stick.

Many women swear by the IUD (Intra-Uterine Device), which is a small, clip-like object that your doctor inserts. While many women report having torrid love affairs with this method, you may experience some extra bleeding, mood swings, and babies—depending on how fertile you are, or as your husband will say, how strong and virile his swimmers happen to be.

If you want to avoid the chemicals and methods that involve a doctor's assistance, then you've got to form an awkwardly intimate relationship with your cervix. Depending on how far up and back it is, by the time you get a sponge or diaphragm in place, you might lose your window of opportunity to actually have sex.

All this is to say that birth control is probably going to be your job. And as your doctor has probably told you, it's an extremely personal choice. But since you've barely got time to read your e-mails let alone a pamphlet at the doctor's office, here's a little cheat sheet with the most important details of each method.

THE MOMINATRIX'S QUICK GUIDE TO BIRTH CONTROL FOR PARENTS		
Method	**Effectiveness**	**Side Effects**
Condom	Think plastic wrap	Brain aneurysm (from trying to figure out how to put it on)
Sponge/Diaphragm	Works if you can get it up there	Panic attacks (from worrying that you won't be able to get it out)
Counting Method	Ha. Hahahahaha.	Babies
Pullout Method	Seriously? Do people still do this?	More babies
Birth Control Pills	Great, if you can remember	A monthly week of insanity
Depo-Provera Shot	Very good	The Freshman 15 (again)
The Patch	Good for average-weight women	A pretty rash
IUD	Excellent	The period that keeps on giving

Throwing in the Towel

If your family is complete, then most birth control methods will suffice. However, you might want to consider the more permanent and lower-maintenance options (aka tubal ligation). The obvious benefit to surgical intervention is that you don't need to remember to swallow, stick, or shove anything down your throat or up your vagina. However, there is cutting, heavy medicating, and the whole "irreversible" nature of the procedure that can turn people off. Saying you're absolutely done having kids is one thing, but completely erasing any chance of ever having any more is another.

If you've decided to take this route, then you might want to look into the less invasive Essure procedure, which requires less recovery time and doesn't involve the actual cutting of the fallopian tubes. It is fairly new, however, so if you don't want to be a guinea pig, you might want to do your research and talk to someone else who's had it done.

On the flip side, many women have taken the stance that because they did the delivery, their husbands should do the sterilization. Seems like a reasonable exchange. Even though there's just no male equivalent to having a baby, getting a vasectomy is about as close as you can get.

If your husband is stepping up to the plate—or knife rather—he should know that the vasectomy is an extremely effective procedure that is completely reversible. You know, in case you change your mind, or if he decides to run off and have kids with your nanny.

MOMINATRIX SAYS

Have your partner talk with a couple of guys who have successfully had the procedure. He's more likely to listen to them than you. Or just offer him lots of oral sex.

Regardless of what your husband might tell you, he will live to screw again in a shorter amount of time than he might guess. And with a weekend full of pain pills, frozen peas (for the sore parts), and a six-pack of beer, he should be at full attention soon.

Whatever your choice, don't leave your birth prevention up to the hand of providence. If you do, expect to be wiping yet another tiny little ass in around forty weeks.

BETTER THAN EVER

It really doesn't matter if you're trying to reproduce again or just enjoying the fruits of your relationship: Sex after kids has the potential to be the hottest you've ever had. There's nothing like making it through the baby tsunami that makes up the early months and years of parenthood to bring two people closer together. Hopefully, you'll discover that it made your relationship and didn't break it.

Having babies can make people do some crazy things. You've gone from carefree sedan owners to a couple of minivan drivers who are sniffing little butts for poop, crying over lost naps, and begging a barely walking and talking human being to eat something other than a few noodles and chicken nuggets. And you did it all together.

But just because you've got diapers stashed in your glove box and the Wiggles in your CD player doesn't mean you don't have your own needs. Considering the challenges and pressures that come with being parents, letting off a little steam and reminding yourselves what it's like to be human again can make the difference between barely surviving and living your life to the fullest.

At the end of the day, it's just you and him trying to keep each other afloat in a gigantic sea of tiny plastic toys. He's watched you push a baby from your body; clearly the mystery is gone. And think of all the gynecological appointments you've endured without even an ounce of alcohol. After all that, reconnecting with each other, trying new things in the bedroom, and expressing what you really want sexually should be a no-brainer. And thank heavens for that.

So stop making excuses. You'd do anything for your children, so why not add sex to the list? Happier moms make better moms. And good, hot sex can make you very, very happy.

APPENDIX A

The Mominatrix's Naughty Mom Registry

Who said all gifts should be for the baby? This handy checklist will help you prepare for sex during pregnancy and after the baby arrives.

Safety
○ Condoms
○ Sponge
○ Diaphragm

Feeding
○ Nipple gloss
○ Edible body paints
○ Chocolate body sauce
○ Hathor Lickeur lubricants
○ Lickable body dust

Crotch Care
○ Hair Care Down There kit
○ Pubic hair razor
○ Feminine wipes
○ Ben-Wa balls—Smart balls

Butt Care
○ Preparation H
○ TUCKS Medicated Pads

Bath Time
○ Rubber ducky sex toy
○ Form 6 toy (waterproof/rechargeable)

○ Vibrating sponge
○ Bath pillow

Cleaning
○ Sex toy wipes
○ Sex toy care and cleaning kit

Toiletries
Lotions
○ Mama Mio
○ Earth Mama Angel Baby
○ Ma Mi Skin Care

Lubes
○ Emerita OH! Warming Lubricant
○ Sliquid Organics Natural

Oils
○ Good Clean Love

Gear
○ Sex swing
○ Ccyell Sex Chair
○ The Liberator
○ Monkey Glider

Bedding
○ Sportsheet Bondage Bedsheet
○ Sex pillow

Room Accessories

○ White noise machine
○ iPod music system
○ Candles

Storage/Organizers

○ Sex night planner
○ Sex toy bag
○ Sex toy box

Toys and Gifts

○ SaSi
○ We-Vibe
○ The Cone
○ Handcuffs

Apparel

○ Pasties
○ Sexy nursing bra and panties
○ Lingerie

Viewing Material

○ *Sex and the City* Complete Box Set
○ Netflix membership
○ Babeland.com's Porn Starter Kit
○ Sheila Kelley's *The "S" Factor*

Reading Material

○ *Position of the Day Playbook*—This book features 366 different sexual positions, including caloric expenditure and possible side effects.

○ *Babyproofing Your Marriage*—Excellent advice on how to stay married after kids by four moms who've been through it themselves.

○ *The Smart Girl's Guide to Porn*—Author Violet Blue offers her expertise on bringing porn into your bedroom.

○ *Love in the Time of Colic*—Sex expert Dr. Ian Kerner teams up with author and "naughty mommy" Heidi Raykeil in this funny, frank book about sex after kids.

○ *Porn for New Moms*—Sometimes porn is in the eye of the beholder, in this case, a bunch of hunky guys doing housework while holding babies.

APPENDIX B

Handy Websites

Lotions and Potions

Mama Mio (*www.mamamio.com*)

Maternity Wear

BellaBand (*www.ingridandisabel.com*)

Isabella Oliver (*www.isabellaoliver.com*)

Chiarakruza (*www.chiarakruza.com*)

Rosie Pope (*www.rosiepope.com*)

Nursing Pillows

The Baby Buddy (*www.thebabybuddy.ca*)

Blessed Nest Organic Nesting Pillow (*http://www .blessednestperch.com*)

My Breast Friend (*www.mybrestfriend.com*)

A real Sex Wedge (*www.liberator.com*)

Nursing Bras

Condessa (*www.condessainc.com*)

Agent Provocateur (*www.agentprovocateur.com*)

Bella Materna (*www.bellamaterna.com*)

Sex Games

Nookii (*www.nookii.com*)

Shaving

Pubic hair razors (*www.personalshavers.com*)

Hair Care Down There kit (*www.haircaredownthere.com*)

Nursing Gowns
BOOB (*www.boobdesign.com*)
Majamas (*www.majamas.com*)
Japanese Weekend (*www.japaneseweekend.com*)

Body Slimmers
Spanx (*www.spanx.com*)

C-Section Underwear
Czela Bellies (*www.czelablue.com*)
C-Panty (*www.cpanty.com*)

Diaper Bags
Nest (*www.nestchildren.com*)
Pinnington (*www.pinningtonbags.com*)
Orla Kiely (*www.orlakiely.com*)
Baby Kaed (*www.babykaed.com*)
The Chaiken Diaper Bag (*www.saksfifthavenue.com*)

Diet and Workout Programs
Weight Watchers (*www.weightwatchers.com*)
Stroller Strides (*www.strollerstrides.com*)
Baby Boot Camp (*www.babybootcamp.com*)

Exercise TV (*www.exercisetv.tv*)

Jillian Michaels's 30 Day Shred (*www.jillianmichaels.com*)

Babysitting Services

Sittercity (*www.sittercity.com*)

Care (*www.care.com*)

Parent-Friendly Sex Toys

The Cone (*www.conezone.org*)

Lipstick vibrator

The tingletip (*www.tingletip.com*)

The Con Rev Vibrating Flashlight

The Vortex Vibrations (*www.vortexvibrations.com*)

Couple's Sex Toys

Vibrating cock ring

We-Vibe (*www.we-vibe.com*)

Remote control vibe

Anal Toys

Anal douche

Butt plug

Anal beads

G-spot stimulator

Lubes

Sliquid Sassy Booty Formula

Good Clean Love (*www.goodcleanlove.com*)

Emerita (*www.emerita.com*)

Mom-Friendly Sex-shops

Babeland *(www.babeland.com)*

Eden Fantasys *(www.edenfantasys.com)*

Good Clean Love *(www.goodcleanlove.com)*

INDEX

ABOUT THE AUTHOR

Kristen Chase hails from a small town in New Jersey where she escaped the accent and the big hair, but not a penchant for water ice and soft pretzels. Her career as a music therapist, textbook author, and college professor landed her in Mississippi by way of Pennsylvania and Michigan, where she met her husb and, an Air Force officer and military pilot.

Chase's surprise pregnancy and subsequent struggle as a new mom was the inspiration for her now widely read blog, *Motherhood Uncensored*, which gained popularity as one of the few Internet voices speaking frankly and humorously about the challenges of motherhood, many of which had to do with sex. Soon after, she was invited to write as *The Mominatrix* in a biweekly column for Imper- fectParent.com, sharing her no-holds- barred opinions about sex for parents.

In lieu of a formal background in giving sex advice, Chase taps into her own experience as a mom who has managed to maintain a healthy sex life and a sense of humor with kids in tow.

She keeps busy as the Publisher and Chief Operating Officer of CoolMomPicks.com, a cheeky shopping blog hailed by *Parents* magazine as "The arbiter of what's cool for the swingset crowd."

She has been a guest on NPR, CBS Atlanta, and NBC's *Today* show. Chase currently resides in Atlanta, Georgia, with her three children and her husband, with whom she still has a lot of sex.